ABT

10/03

ALLIED FORCES

By John Hamilton

VISIT US AT
WWW.ABDOPUB.COM

Published by ABDO & Daughters, an imprint of ABDO Publishing Company, 4940 Viking Drive, Suite 622, Edina, Minnesota 55435.

Printed in the United States.

Edited by: Tamara L. Britton and Kate A. Conley
Graphic Design: Arturo Leyva, David Bullen
Cover Design: Castaneda Dunham, Inc.
Photos: British Ministry of Defence, Corbis

Library of Congress Cataloging-in-Publication Data

Hamilton, John, 1959-
    Allied forces / John Hamilton.
      p. cm. -- (War in Iraq)
    Includes index.
    Summary: Describes the coalition of forty-eight countries which supported the 2003 military action against Iraq, detailing the efforts of the forces provided by the United States, Great Britain, and a handful of other countries.
    ISBN 1-59197-491-7
  1. Iraq War, 2003--Juvenile literature. [1. Iraq War, 2003.] I. Title. II. Series.

    DS79.76.H36 2003
    956.7044'3--dc22

                                   2003052471

WAR ★ IRAQ

TABLE OF CONTENTS

U.S. president George W. Bush and Secretary of State Colin Powell sought worldwide support to remove Saddam Hussein from power.

COALITION OF THE WILLING

When the United States went to war with Iraq in the spring of 2003, it didn't go alone. Though U.S. troops carried out the lion's share of combat, the United Kingdom (U.K.) also played a key role in defeating Saddam Hussein's brutal regime. A small group of Australians were also sent into harm's way, as were special operations troops from Poland.

Some nations criticized the United States for invading Iraq with such a small group of supporters, far fewer than the 1991 Persian Gulf War. The U.S. State Department, led by Secretary of State Colin Powell, tried to show that there was worldwide support for the war. To do this, Powell listed a group of 30 countries whose leaders agreed that Saddam Hussein had to be removed from power to make the world safer.

After making phone calls, President George W. Bush and Powell were able to persuade the 30 countries, called the Coalition of the Willing, to make their support public. Powell added,

"There are 15 other nations who for one reason or another do not yet wish to be publicly named but will be supporting the coalition." In fact, by the end of March 2003, the White House announced that 48 countries had joined the coalition, all pledging support in one form or another.

Some of the nations in the coalition offered combat troops, equipment, or logistical and intelligence support. Others guaranteed fly-over rights to coalition warplanes, or humanitarian and reconstruction aid to postwar Iraq.

Many countries found it politically difficult to declare support for the coalition, preferring instead to give quiet help when needed. For example, several Arab countries joined the coalition, but they felt pressured to keep the news secret for fear of angering their people, most of whom were against the war. Even countries such as Qatar and Bahrain, which had a large American military presence during the war, tried to downplay their support. The countries that publicly declared their support faced a backlash at home. And the U.S. State Department admitted that only a handful would be sending actual troops into the combat zone. Secretary of State Powell said, "I hope that they will all be able to do everything that is possible within their means to support the coalition militarily, diplomatically, politically and economically."

6

ALLIED FORCES

COALITION OF THE WILLING

Afghanistan

Albania

Angola

Australia

Azerbaijan

Bulgaria

Colombia

Costa Rica

The Czech Republic

Denmark

Dominican Republic

El Salvador

Eritrea

Estonia

Ethiopia

Georgia

Honduras

Hungary

Iceland

Italy

Japan

Kuwait

Latvia

Lithuania

Macedonia

Marshall Islands

Micronesia

Mongolia

The Netherlands

Nicaragua

Palau

Panama

The Philippines

Poland

Portugal

Romania

Rwanda

Singapore

Slovakia

Solomon Islands

South Korea

Spain

Tonga

Turkey

Uganda

Ukraine

The United Kingdom

The United States

Uzbekistan

48 countries joined the United States to form the Coalition of the Willing

The list of countries supporting the war was notable because it didn't include several traditional U.S. allies. For example, France and Germany remained opposed to the war, and refused to help remove Saddam from power. Countries opposed to the war had many reasons. Some believed that the United Nations (UN) needed more time to uncover Iraqi weapons of mass destruction. Other nations didn't want to risk their economic ties to Iraq, especially its oil industry. Some countries wanted to oppose the United States because they believe it wields too much power in international affairs. Other countries were simply opposed to war of any kind.

Despite the deep reservations of many countries, and over the objection of the UN, the United States was able to assemble a core group of friends willing to help topple Saddam's regime. The United Kingdom contributed about 45,000 troops. Australia sent 2,000 soldiers to the area, and Poland sent 200. A handful of other countries also sent troops to be used in noncombat support roles, such as military police. Fearing an Iraqi attack using weapons of mass destruction, some countries also sent chemical and biological decontamination teams.

The Bush administration tried to deflect criticism that the coalition was comprised of a very narrow group of allies that bowed to U.S. political and military power. A White House briefing stated

ALLIED FORCES

that "it is no accident that many member nations of the coalition recently escaped from the boot of a tyrant or have felt the scourge of terrorism. All coalition member nations understand the threat Saddam Hussein's weapons pose to the world and the devastation his regime has wreaked on the Iraqi people." The administration pointed out that the population of coalition countries totals approximately 1.23 billion people, representing nearly every major race, religion, and ethnicity in the world.

With its allied forces behind it, the United States began military operations in Iraq on March 19, 2003. As bombs began falling on Baghdad, President Bush addressed the American public. Coalition forces, he explained, were in the "early stages of military operations to disarm Iraq, to free its people and to defend the world from grave danger."

THE UNITED KINGDOM

By far the biggest supporter of the United States in the war in Iraq was its longtime ally, the United Kingdom. For the U.S. military, the war in Iraq was code-named Operation Iraqi Freedom. For British troops, the war was dubbed Operation *Telic*. *Telic* is a Greek term that means "expressing purpose."

On March 20, the day after operations against Iraq officially began, British prime minister Tony Blair spoke to his nation. "On Tuesday night," he said, "I gave the order for British forces to take part in military action in Iraq. Tonight, British servicemen and women are engaged from air, land and sea. Their mission: to remove Saddam Hussein from power, and disarm Iraq of its weapons of mass destruction. . . . Should terrorists obtain these weapons now being manufactured and traded round the world, the carnage they could inflict to our economies, our security, to world peace would be beyond our most vivid imagination. My judgment, as Prime Minister, is that this threat is real, growing and of an

British prime minister Tony Blair addresses the media, promising to help the United States end Saddam Hussein's reign of terror.

U.K. ARMED FORCES

Royal Navy logo

British Army logo

Royal Air Force logo

entirely different nature to any conventional threat to our security that Britain has faced before."

Operation *Telic* consisted of air, land, and sea forces. The United Kingdom sent, or deployed, approximately 45,000 servicemen and women to the Persian Gulf region to fight against Iraq. This number represented nearly 30 percent of Britain's total armed forces personnel.

The U.K.'s armed forces are divided into three main groups: the Royal Navy, the British Army, and the Royal Air Force (RAF).

THE ROYAL NAVY

To defend its shores, and to project power to its interests in foreign lands, the United Kingdom has depended on a strong navy for hundreds of years. Before the age of flight, naval power was often an important reason why some nations succeeded in war and others did not.

In the last part of the sixteenth century, England and Spain were seafaring rivals. Spain was one of the strongest countries in international politics. With its formidable navy, it wielded power and colonized territory all over the known world. In addition to political friction between the countries, King Philip II vowed to conquer the island nation and convert its people, most of whom were Protestants, to Roman Catholicism.

In 1588, Spain sent a huge fleet of ships across the English Channel. The fleet was called the Invincible Armada, and was comprised of 130 ships. It was supposed to join another armada coming from the Spanish Netherlands, but that group never arrived. English ships harassed the Spanish for more than a week, firing at their flanks as they sailed along the English Channel. The English, commanded by Lord Thomas Howard and Sir Francis Drake, were careful not to directly confront the Spanish in close fighting, fearing the more powerful ships of the line.

On July 28, 1588, the English sent fire ships—old vessels filled with burning tar and gunpowder—into the Spanish line, scattering the armada. The next day, at the Battle of Gravelines, the English picked apart the Spanish fleet.

The Spanish commander, the Duke of Medina-Sidonia, canceled the invasion and turned north to flee from the English ships. For three days the English pursued the Spaniards, returning home only after running out of ammunition. To make matters worse for the Spanish, rough seas punished the fleet as it rounded the coast of Scotland, sending many ships to the bottom of the ocean.

When it was all over, the surviving Spanish ships limped back to their homeports. Their defeat at the hands of the English navy was humiliating and demoralizing. Seventy Spanish ships were destroyed, and many more were severely damaged. Nearly 15,000 men perished. It was a disaster for the Spanish, who would never again dominate the seas. For England, the battle was the beginning of its rise as a great seafaring nation. For hundreds of years afterward, the United Kingdom wielded its power in international affairs, spearheaded by its powerful navy.

Even today, in the age of airplanes, the United Kingdom's Royal Navy is an important part of its armed forces. That's because water covers almost 71 percent of the world, and two-thirds of the world's population lives within 100 miles (161 km) of the coast. The United Kingdom has approximately 10,500 miles (16,898 km) of coastline to defend. The country is the world's sixth-largest trading nation, and most of its goods are transported by sea. Its fleet is the thirteenth largest in the world. With so much at stake on the high seas, the United Kingdom continues to rely on a strong navy to protect its shores and its interests abroad. The Royal Navy includes a variety of sophisticated ships and submarines to carry out these tasks.

For Operation *Telic*, the Royal Navy deployed Naval Task Group 2003. This force included the aircraft carrier HMS *Ark Royal*, a helicopter carrier, several destroyers and frigates, support vessels, and a fleet submarine armed with cruise missiles. In addition, the navy sent an amphibious force of 4,000 rapid-response Royal Marines. Together with 2,000 U.S. Marines, these commandos staged a strike on the Iraqi port city of Basra. It was the largest joint operation since World War II.

The Royal Navy currently has three aircraft carriers in its fleet. All are categorized as Invincible-class aircraft carriers. The HMS *Ark Royal* is larger than her two sister ships, the HMS *Invincible*

NAVAL TASK GROUP 2003

Ships from the British Naval Task Group 2003 move into position in the Mediterranean Sea.

and HMS *Illustrious*. Built in 1978, the ship is 683 feet (208 m) long. It is powered by four gasoline turbine engines, which give it a maximum speed of approximately 30 knots or 35 miles (56 km) per hour. It carries 1,001 ship's company, along with 320 air group personnel.

Aircraft carriers from the United Kingdom are smaller than the supercarriers built by the U.S. Navy. Another difference is the ski jump built at the front of the ship. This ramp helps give airplanes extra lift as they are catapulted off the flight deck. The *Ark Royal*'s ski jump is steeper than that of either the *Invincible* or the *Illustrious*.

The *Ark Royal* is used as a flagship, which means it leads the naval task group. Aircraft carriers are very powerful weapons. They can be deployed almost anywhere in the world, in international waters, and can project force far inland with planes, helicopters, and Marine commandos. The *Ark Royal* uses Royal Air Force Harrier GR7 ground attack jump jets, which are escorted by Sea Harrier FA2 fighter/attack aircraft. They can also carry out antisubmarine warfare using Sea King Mk 4 helicopters. Sea King Mk 4 helicopters are used to ferry Royal Marine commando units to shore. The *Ark Royal* can also deploy Chinook support helicopters if a mission calls for heavier lifting capacity.

The Royal Marines, which are part of the Royal Navy, are one of the oldest units in the British armed forces. They were formed in 1664, and have won many battle honors in nearly three and one-half centuries of active duty.

The United Kingdom describes the Royal Marines as a "go anywhere" amphibious force, and a key part of the government's Rapid Reaction Force. These commandos undergo rigorous training to prepare them for combat anywhere in the world, including deserts, mountains, and jungles. They are similar to U.S. Marines in their training and combat experience.

Also deployed in Naval Task Group 2003 was the amphibious helicopter carrier HMS *Ocean*. Launched in 1995, the *Ocean* provides rapid assault capability to the task group. The ship carries an Embarked Military Force (EMF), which are troops accompanied by 12 medium support helicopters, 6 attack helicopters, and 4 landing craft vehicles.

Three Type 42 destroyers were used in the war against Iraq. The Royal Navy considers these the backbone of its antiair capability. Each of the destroyers—the HMS *Liverpool*, the HMS *Edinburgh*, and the HMS *York*—are equipped with the Sea Dart medium-range air defense missile system. The Sea Dart provides air defense to an entire group of ships, in this case the aircraft carrier battle group. Sea Dart missiles have an effective range of

more than 50 miles (80 km). A solid fuel booster engine gives the missile a speed of more than Mach 2 before it leaves the launcher arm. In addition to antiair defense, British destroyers carry out patrol and boarding operations.

Other ships in Naval Task Group 2003 included minesweepers, such as the HMS *Grimsby* and the HMS *Ledbury*. These ships kept ports and coastal shipping lanes free of mines. These special ships have hulls made of glass-reinforced plastic, rather than steel, which could set off a mine. They are equipped with high-definition sonar and unmanned robot submarines called Remote Controlled Mine Disposal System Vehicles (RCMDS). In addition, they carry standard sweep gear that trails behind the ships searching for mines. Minesweepers can detect mines on the bottom of the ocean, or in mid-water, by bouncing sound waves off them and detecting the echo. RCMDS can then be guided to the mines, which are destroyed with high explosives.

In addition to a variety of other support vessels, the naval task group also included one Fleet Submarine equipped with Tomahawk land attack cruise missiles, which have a range of more than 1,151 miles (1,852 km). Fleet Submarine is another term for Ship Submersible Nuclear (SSN). These subs can act independently, providing stealthy attack capability when needed, but they often accompany surface ship task groups to give protection against enemy submarines.

Royal Marines look seaward from the top of a nuclear-powered Fleet Submarine.

The two main groups of SSNs in the Royal Navy are the Swiftsure- and the Trafalgar-class. They are high-speed, deep-diving subs that can carry out a flexible range of missions. In addition to land attack and antisubmarine operations, SSNs are good at seeking out and destroying enemy submarines using British spearfish torpedoes or Sub Harpoon missiles, which can hit the enemy from a distance of more than 50 miles (80 km). British attack subs are also commonly used to spy on enemy forces, and to deploy Special Forces teams onto hostile shores.

The United Kingdom also maintains a fleet of Vanguard-class Ship Submersible Ballistic Nuclear (SSBN) submarines. These fearsome machines have 16 missile tubes that can fire Trident II D5 nuclear missiles, with a range of more than 4,603 miles (7,408 km). Each missile can deliver up to 12 warheads, which allows several targets to be struck with a single missile. These submarines threaten potential enemies with swift and immediate destruction. The United Kingdom hopes that this will deter future aggression against its homeland.

Vanguard-class submarines are high-speed, long-endurance
underwater vessels that are powered by nuclear energy.

THE BRITISH ARMY

For thousands of years the British Isles have suffered through invasions, occupations, and civil war. The land has seen a continual series of conflicts, from Roman legionnaires to plundering Vikings and conquering Normans.

Even so, most British people don't see themselves as a warlike people. Historically, they have considered armies to be needed only at times of conflict, to be reduced or disbanded in peacetime. The military draft, or conscription, has been used only twice in the nation's history, both during the twentieth century, at times of national emergency. By not relying on huge standing armies, and because of the need to support the outposts of its worldwide empire, the British armed forces have remained relatively small. This has influenced British military strategy, which relies on superior tactics and smart fighting to outwit and outfight the enemy, even when outnumbered. Great Britain also relies on alliances with other countries when fighting major wars.

The British Army has a long and colorful history. The oldest unit in continuous existence is the Honourable Artillery Company, which received its charter in 1537 by King Henry VIII. Another unit, the Royal Monmouthshire Royal Engineers, was established in 1539. It wasn't until the eighteenth century, however, that the British Army gained recognition as a fighting power that demanded respect. Between 1704 and 1712, John Churchill, the first Duke of Marlborough, expanded the army and won several important victories over the French and their allies.

Today, the British Army is still organized using the regiment system. Each regiment has its own history and tradition. According to the National Army Museum in London, "Over the years this system has established a feeling of service, comradeship and regimental pride which lies at the very heart of the Army's fighting spirit and has frequently been a major factor in enabling the British Army to prevail, sometimes against impossible odds or in conditions of extreme hardship."

The land forces of Operation *Telic* numbered approximately 26,000 personnel. Working closely with American forces, the British troops fought several key battles in Iraq. This included the battle for the port city of Basra, which involved special operations troops, tank battles, parachute drops, and helicopter

Images of the Challenger 2 tank

attacks. Several famous British units were involved in the Iraqi war, including the Black Watch, the Royal Scots Dragoon Guards, and the Seventh Armoured Brigade, also known as the Desert Rats.

British forces use some of the most advanced weapons systems available today. The Challenger 2 is the British Army's main battle tank. Approximately 120 Challenger 2 tanks were sent to Iraq to fight in Operation *Telic*. They were a key weapon used during the battle for control of the city of Basra.

The Challenger 2 is a huge, powerful machine, comparable to the U.S. Army's Abrams M1A1 main battle tank. The Challenger's turret mounts a 120mm L30 gun, which is very effective at destroying enemy tanks. The turret is also armed with a 7.62mm chain gun for firing at troops and light-armored vehicles, and a 7.62mm GPMG machine gun for air defense. The Challenger is protected by highly successful Chobham armor, which defends against most antitank weapons. Its crew of four includes a commander, gunner, ammo loader, and driver. The Challenger measures 27.2 feet (8.3 m) long, 11.5 feet (3.5 m) wide, and weighs 68.89 tons (62.5 tonnes). It is fitted with a 12-cylinder Rolls-Royce engine, and can sustain a maximum road speed of 35 miles per hour (56 km/h).

British forces also used the Warrior. It is an infantry fighting vehicle, used to quickly transport troops into battle. Armed with a 30mm Rarden cannon and a coaxial 7.62mm Hughes chain gun, it is also used to support the Challenger 2 main battle tank. The Warrior is fast and highly mobile, even over rough terrain. Fully loaded at 27 tons (24 tonnes), the Warrior can carry a crew of three, plus seven soldiers, into battle at a road speed of 47 miles per hour (76 km/h). It measures 20.8 feet (6.34 m) long and 9.8 feet (3 m) wide. The Warrior is hardened against nuclear, biological, and chemical weapons, and includes a full range of night-vision equipment. Approximately 150 Warrior fighting vehicles took part in Operation *Telic*.

For artillery in the war with Iraq, the British Army relied mainly on the 105mm Light Gun, a relatively lightweight field artillery piece. Weighing just two tons (1.8 tonnes), it can be carried around the battlefield slung from Puma or Chinook helicopters. With a crew of six, it can fire high explosives, smoke, and target-marking ammunition at a rate of fire of up to six rounds per minute, at a maximum range of approximately 10.7 miles (17.2 km). Because it is so easily transportable, it is often used by parachute and commando field artillery regiments.

The Lynx is the British Army's main antitank helicopter. It carries eight TOW antitank guided missiles, plus two to four

ALLIED FORCES

7.62mm machine guns. It uses sophisticated sighting and tracking electronics to find and destroy enemy targets. It has a maximum speed of 205 miles per hour (330 km/h), with a range of approximately 52.8 miles (85 km). The Lynx has a crew of one pilot and one air-gunner/observer. Without its antitank weapons system, the Lynx is sometimes used as a utility helicopter in a variety of missions, including reconnaissance.

The British Army relies on the Gazelle helicopter mainly for observation and reconnaissance. It is especially useful in antitank operations, and can be used as an air observation post, or forward air controller for other aircraft. The Gazelle is also used to evacuate wounded soldiers, carry passengers, and relay communications. It has a range of 416 miles (669 km), and can attain a maximum speed of 165 miles per hour (266 km/h). It can be armed with two 7.62mm machine guns, although this is not a standard fitting.

The Lynx helicopter

The Gazelle helicopter

THE ROYAL AIR FORCE

On April 1, 1918, during World War I, Britain's Royal Flying Corps and Royal Naval Air Service merged into one central flying command, the Royal Air Force (RAF). Since that time, the British air service has been a pioneer in the development of combat aircraft, from the Spitfires of the Battle of Britain in World War II, to the Harrier jump jets of today.

During Operation *Telic*, the RAF sent a package of approximately 100 fixed-wing aircraft to Iraq as part of the Sixteenth Air Assault Brigade, which included approximately 7,000 RAF personnel. The aircraft included Hercules transport planes, refueling planes, and helicopters. The backbone of the force, however, was comprised of the RAF's trio of Harrier, Jaguar, and Tornado jet fighters.

The original Harrier was first used in the 1960s. Since then, it has been upgraded with improved weaponry and advanced guidance systems. It is so versatile in combat that the United States

eventually designed its own version, the AV-8B Harrier II, which is the model on which the Harrier GR7 is based.

The Harrier GR7 is the latest version of the RAF's jump jet. It can take off and land vertically, like a helicopter. It can also fly forward like a conventional jet, reaching speeds of up to 661 miles per hour (1,064 km/h). It is ideal for operating from ships at sea or recently captured and unprepared airstrips in enemy territory.

The Harrier GR7 can be used both day and night. At night, it uses forward-looking infrared (FLIR) equipment together with the pilot's night-vision goggles, which give it a major advantage over any enemy without night-vision equipment. Harriers are designed to work best at low level and at subsonic speeds, but they can also fly high in the sky at faster speeds against enemy aircraft. The Harrier's main role in battle, however, is to attack at low or medium level, using smart or dumb bombs, and to provide close-air support to British ground forces if they are under attack.

Harrier GR7s have a wingspan of 30 feet, 4 inches (9.25 m), and a length of 46 feet, 4 inches (14.12 m). They are armed with two 25mm cannons, and up to 16 Mk 82 or 6 Mk 83 bombs. They can also be fitted with Maverick air to ground missiles, Paveway laser-guided bombs, Sidewinder air-to-air missiles, Brimstone antiarmor missiles, or CRV-7 rocket pods.

From top to bottom: a Jaguar, a Harrier GR7, and a Tornado GR4

Jaguars are multirole aircraft that can fight against enemy planes. They can also be used as bomber and ground attack aircraft. They were originally intended as training aircraft, but the RAF fitted them with major avionics upgrades that make them a potent offensive force. They are also used in a reconnaissance role to find an enemy's force level and position. They use an externally mounted pod that takes images and video, together with a digital moving map display.

Jaguars have a wingspan of 28 feet, 6 inches (8.69 m), and a length of 55 feet, 2 inches (16.82 m). They can reach speeds of up to 1,056 miles per hour (1,699 km/h). They are armed with two 30mm Aden guns and up to 10,000 pounds (4,536 kg) of other weapons, which might include cluster bombs, Paveway laser-guided bombs, Sidewinder air-to-air missiles, or CRV-7 rockets, depending on the mission.

The Tornado GR4 is the RAF's main ground attack aircraft. It specializes in supersonic flight, close to the ground. Its main job is to penetrate enemy territory and drop smart bombs on targets.

The Tornado was developed in the late 1960s as a joint project between the United Kingdom, Germany, and Italy. The GR4 upgrade now includes night-vision capability, improved cockpit controls, and Sky Shadow radar jamming pods. Its main flight

system and navigation computer takes advantage of Global Positioning System (GPS) data.

Tornado aircraft have a wingspan of 45 feet, 7 inches (13.9 m), and a length of 54 feet, 10 inches (16.7 m). They have a maximum speed of 1,452 miles per hour (2,337 km/h), or Mach 2.2. They are armed with one Mauser 27mm cannon and up to 18,000 pounds (8,165 kg) of bombs and missiles, depending on the mission. These might include cluster bombs, Brimstone antiarmor missiles, or Sidewinder air-to-air missiles.

A Tornado F3 flies over Iraq during Operation *Telic*.

Armed with Sidewinder and Skyflash missiles, a Tornado aircraft ascends into the sky.

OTHER ARMED FORCES

In addition to the United States and the United Kingdom, a handful of other countries sent their armed forces as part of the coalition to free Iraq from the dictatorship of Saddam Hussein. Some countries, including the Eastern European nations of Hungary and the Czech Republic, allowed allied planes to use airbases, or offered army personnel who specialized in combating chemical weapons.

In addition, Poland sent approximately 200 chemical warfare specialists to work alongside U.S. troops. They were available to clean up chemical spills in drinking water supplies, but were not actually used. Poland also sent 54 soldiers from its elite GROM special operations unit. These were the only Eastern European soldiers actually involved in ground operations in Iraq. They worked with U.S. Navy SEALs to secure Iraqi oil fields during the opening days of the war.

Australia also committed a sizable force to the coalition. On March 18, 2003, Prime Minister John Howard announced that

ALLIED FORCES

approximately 2,000 Australian troops would contribute to the war in Iraq. In a March 20 speech to the Australian people, Howard said, "The government has decided to commit Australian forces to action to disarm Iraq because we believe it is right, it is lawful and it's in Australia's national interest.

"We are determined to join other countries to deprive Iraq of its weapons of mass destruction, its chemical and biological weapons, which even in minute quantities are capable of causing death and destruction on a mammoth scale."

Dubbed Operation Falconer by the Australian Defence Force, the military contribution included Royal Australian Navy frigates HMA *Anzac* and *Darwin*, a mine-clearing team, and two P-3C Orion maritime patrol aircraft. A squadron of 14 F/A-18 Royal Australian Air Force Hornet fighter aircraft were also deployed. These are very similar to the Hornets used by U.S. forces. Operation Falconer also included a Special Forces Task Group that had about 500 personnel, including specially trained commandos who dealt with the threat of weapons of mass destruction. Other Australian Special Forces teams were sent into Iraq before the official start of the war, but for reasons of national security, their exact role could not be revealed.

In addition to Special Forces activity and F/A-18 Hornet combat missions, the Australian Navy saw action on March 24, as

OPERATION FALCONER

A squadron of Australian F/A-18A planes awaits mid-air refueling during a training exercise in preparation for Operation Falconer.

Aussie naval gunfire destroyed Iraqi coastal defensive positions. An artillery battery and bunkers were also hit. Brigadier Maurie McNarn, commander of Australian forces in the Middle East, said, "Australia's contribution to the coalition, while a niche force, is designed to be potent, effective, and leading edge."

Shortly after the war with Iraq was completed, the United States announced that several other countries would contribute combat-ready patrols to bring stability to the country. In addition to U.S. and British forces, eight other countries agreed to send peacekeeping troops—Poland, Italy, Spain, Ukraine, Denmark, Bulgaria, Albania, and the Netherlands. The Philippines, South Korea, Qatar, and Australia agreed to provide noncombat forces, whose duties would include searching for weapons of mass destruction, and destroying unexploded bombs. The major nations that opposed the United States in freeing Iraq—France, Germany, and Russia—were not asked to contribute peacekeeping forces.

WEB SITES
WWW.ABDOPUB.COM

To learn more about allied forces, visit ABDO Publishing Company on the World Wide Web at **www.abdopub.com**. Web sites about allied forces are featured on our Book Links page. These links are routinely monitored and updated to provide the most current information available.

A British armored military convoy rolls into Iraq.

TIMELINE

1537
Oldest British army unit in continuous existence received charter from King Henry VIII

1588
Battle of Gravelines marked the end of Spain's domination of the seas. England's domination of the seas began

1664
British Royal Marines formed

1704–1712
First Duke of Marlborough expanded the British army

1918
April 1: British Royal Flying Corps and Royal Naval Air Service merged into one central flying command, the Royal Air Force

1960s
Original Harrier first used

1991
Persian Gulf War

2003
March 18: Australian prime minister John Howard pledged approximately 2,000 Australian troops to fight alongside coalition forces in Iraq

March 19: United States began military operations in Iraq

March 20: British prime minister Tony Blair announced his country's involvement in the Iraq war

FAST FACTS

- By the end of March 2003, the White House announced that 48 countries had joined the Coalition of the Willing.

- The United Kingdom sent about 45,000 troops to support the allied effort. Australia sent about 2,000 soldiers and Poland sent 200.

- The war in Iraq was code-named Operation Iraqi Freedom by the U.S. military. British troops called it Operation *Telic*, and the Australian Defence Force dubbed it Operation Falconer.

- The British Royal Navy guards the United Kingdom's 10,500 miles (16,898 km) of coastline.

- The Royal Navy deployed Naval Task Group 2003 for Operation *Telic*. This task group included an aircraft carrier, a helicopter carrier, several destroyers and frigates, support vessels, and a Fleet Submarine armed with cruise missiles. An amphibious force of 4,000 rapid-response Royal Marines was also part of this group.

- Four thousand Royal Marines together with 2,000 U.S. Marines staged a strike on the Iraqi port city of Basra. This was the largest joint operation since World War II.

- British aircraft carriers are smaller than the supercarriers built by the U.S. Navy.

- The Royal Marines are part of the Royal Navy and are one of the oldest units in the British military.

- Poland sent about 200 chemical warfare specialists to work alongside U.S. troops. The country also sent 54 soldiers from its elite GROM special operations unit.

ALLIED FORCES

GLOSSARY

amphibious
Operating on both land and water.

avionics
Electronics that are designed for use in aerospace vehicles.

casualty
A soldier or civilian who is injured or killed in an act of war.

deter
To prevent or discourage an action from occurring.

Mach 2
Twice the speed of sound.

munitions
Generally, munitions refer to all war supplies, but mainly refer to bombs and ammunition.

reconnaissance
Finding the location of the enemy. Reconnaissance missions help commanders decide which forces to send into enemy territory.

smart bomb
A bomb or missile that navigates its way to a target, usually by following a laser beam "painted" on the target by a plane or special operations soldier on the ground. Smart bombs are very accurate.

supersonic
Faster than the speed of sound, which travels at 1,116 feet per second (340 m/sec).

warhead
The forward section of a bomb or missile usually containing an explosive charge. Warheads can also be filled with chemical or biological agents.

INDEX

ALLIED FORCES

to David

a small token
for being such
a good listener.

Orly

THE ARCHAEOLOGY OF ANCIENT EGYPT

A BODLEY HEAD ARCHAEOLOGY

The Archaeology of Ancient Egypt

T. G. H. JAMES

Drawings by
ROSEMONDE NAIRAC

THE BODLEY HEAD · London Sydney Toronto

UNIFORM WITH THIS BOOK

MAGNUS MAGNUSSON *Introducing Archaeology*
RONALD HARKER *Digging Up The Bible Lands*

IN PREPARATION

REYNOLD HIGGINS *Minoan Crete*
HUMPHREY CASE *The Dawn of European Civilisation*
MAGNUS MAGNUSSON *Viking Expansion Westward*

FRONTISPIECE
The solid gold third
coffin of King
Tutankhamun

THIS BOOK IS FOR STEPHEN

Printed and bound in Great Britain for
The Bodley Head Ltd
9 Bow Street, London WC2E 7AL
by William Clowes & Sons Ltd, Beccles
Set in Monophoto Ehrhardt by
BAS Printers Limited, Wallop, Hampshire
First published 1972

CONTENTS

ACKNOWLEDGMENTS

Thanks are due to the following for permission to reproduce black and white photographs: the Griffith Institute, Ashmolean Museum, Oxford, frontispiece, 77, 78, 81, 83, 85; Peter Clayton, pages 8, 15, 18, 23, 39, 68, 88, 104, 111, 133; the Trustees of the British Museum, pages 14, 90, 94, 122; Department of Antiquities, Ashmolean Museum, Oxford, page 24; United Arab Republic (Egypt) Tourist Information Centre, pages 31, 34, 36, 42, 99, 108, 130; Museum of Fine Arts, Boston, Massachusetts, pages 45, 46, 51; Roger Wood, pages 53, 135, 138; the Egyptian Expedition, the Metropolitan Museum of Art, New York, pages 57, 58, 61, 63; Dr Labib Habachi, pages 65, 72; Radio Times Hulton Picture Library, page 75; the Louvre Museum, Paris, page 125.

Thanks are due to the following for permission to reproduce coloured photographs: Peter Clayton, jacket, facing pages 32 (*top*), 49, 113 (*top* and *bottom*), 129 (*bottom*); the Trustees of the British Museum, facing page 48 (*top*); the Egyptian Expedition, the Metropolitan Museum of Art, New York, facing page 48 (*bottom*); UNESCO, Paris, facing page 128 (*bottom*).

PREFACE

The history of Egypt began more than five thousand years ago, but the scientific study of its ancient remains, usually called Egyptology, was born only one hundred and fifty years ago. In September 1822, a brilliant young French scholar, Jean-François Champollion, presented to the Academy in Paris the first results of his decipherment of Egyptian hieroglyphics. From that moment knowledge about ancient Egypt began to grow, and over the years scholars of all kinds have contributed to this growth.

Among these scholars, the ones who have made the most dramatic discoveries are the excavators. Even before Champollion published his momentous results, there were people working in the field in Egypt, examining the visible monuments, and making attempts at a kind of excavation. One of the most notable of the early 'excavators' was a man called Giovanni Belzoni. In his methods and attitudes he was fairly typical of the treasure-seekers who raided ancient sites in Egypt in the early nineteenth century. His principal aim was to find fine things, chiefly pieces of sculpture, which would enhance the private collection of his patron, or in time enter a public museum. To this end he was not too particular about the methods he used; quick results were his ideal, and if some ancient material were destroyed in the recovery of a royal statue, that was of little concern to him.

But Belzoni and his contemporaries were to a large extent working in the dark. They could not read the inscriptions in the tombs they discovered, or the names carved on the statues they unearthed. Of all ancient peoples the Egyptians were the most obsessed by the written word. A statue without a name represented

7

nobody; a building without a text was meaningless. So everything was inscribed with informative texts, written in the peculiar Egyptian script called hieroglyphics. Until hieroglyphics were deciphered, students of antiquity could only have a faint inkling of the history and life of the ancient Egyptians.

When this water colour of the Ramesseum at Thebes was painted in the first half of the nineteenth century by the English artist David Roberts excavators were still able to remove large quantities of Egyptian sculpture.

A scientific approach to excavation was to come only slowly as excavators appreciated more and more that their task was not simply one of recovering buried treasure, but also of retrieving information about the past.

The principal purpose of this book is to show how excavation has contributed to the advance of the study of ancient Egypt. Particular excavations have been chosen, partly to illustrate the methods used by famous excavators, but chiefly to show how the history of Egypt has been illuminated by the discoveries made at certain places. The successive chapters, following the course of Egyptian history, describe how some of the great discoveries have been made and how others, not so spectacular, have contributed to the better understanding of obscure periods. In the discoveries all kinds of Egyptologists take part: excavators who dig things up, archaeologists who study the finds of excavators, linguists who read inscriptions, and 'arm-chair' scholars who put together and interpret the discoveries of others. All these different kinds of scholar have their parts to play in building up the story of an ancient people.

8

1

The Outline of
Egyptian History

In the fifth century BC a Greek writer from Halicarnassus in Asia Minor travelled to Egypt to collect background material for the history of the Persian Wars which he was preparing. His name was Herodotus, and he is often called the 'Father of History'. The book he eventually wrote was lively and informative; he had collected his material carefully, asking good questions and listening with attention. In Egypt, working through interpreters, or gleaning his facts from Greek residents in the country, he collected a very miscellaneous body of information. He had no way of checking what he was told, and, being very partial to a good story, he readily noted down tales about the ancient kings of Egypt which owed more to romance than truth. With greater knowledge today it is possible to distinguish truth from romance in Herodotus' work. His facts are often right, more often nearly right, and occasionally wildly wrong. Sometimes it is possible to see where he has misunderstood his informants; sometimes he has gone wrong because he has tried to iron out implausible elements in stories—things which he felt could not have happened. But in general he is not a bad source for Egyptian history, only an inadequate one.

The Greeks were fascinated by Egypt, but they were very ill-informed about the country and, in particular, its history. The inadequacy of their knowledge probably reflected to a great extent the casual attitude of the Egyptians themselves to their own history. As far as is known, the Egyptians of the great periods of antiquity did not write narrative histories of the kind we are now accustomed to read. Lists of kings were preserved in temple and royal archives; if the list was properly prepared it contained lengths of reigns as well as names. But when a list was carved on the walls of a temple it only contained names. Such lists scarcely provided the bare skeleton of a history, especially as they were usually edited so that unmemorable or unworthy kings were not included.

Before hieroglyphics were deciphered the king-lists could not be used by modern writers on Egyptian history. They relied mostly on the works of Herodotus and of other Greek writers who inserted sections on Egypt into their histories of the ancient world. There was, however, another work, compiled directly from ancient Egyptians sources, including king-lists, which was altogether more trustworthy as a source. This was the history written by Manetho, an Egyptian priest, who lived in the third century BC. Modern scholars did not at first regard it very highly because it had only survived in a very abbreviated form, and in this form it did not possess the narrative qualities of Herodotus' history. In due course, however, modern scholars began to see that Manetho's history could increasingly be proved reliable as hieroglyphic records were discovered and translated.

Manetho undoubtedly had good records to consult when he prepared his work. Even so, it must not be forgotten that he wrote at a time when the idea of careful, accurate history as we understand it today was not well appreciated. Some stories preserved in the fragments are just as romantically mythical as ones found in Herodotus. He also began his history with an account of Egypt's supposed earliest history when it was thought that the land was ruled first by gods and then by demi-gods.

For the story of the time when human rulers reigned over the land of Egypt, Manetho organised the kings into groups which he called dynasties. From the beginning to the end of Egyptian history there were thirty dynasties. The first king of the first dynasty was called Menes. He qualified for this position because he was the first king to establish his rule over the whole of Egypt. Early historians who were unwilling to accept the authority of Manetho's history were ready to adopt his division of the kings of Egypt into thirty dynasties. Manetho's dynasties are not quite the same as the dynasties of English history, like the Tudors, the Stuarts and the Hanoverians. Changes of dynasty did not, apparently, coincide always with changes of ruling houses. Sometimes the change seems to have been marked by some important political act, by the break-down of central government, by the emergence of a particularly powerful king. Nevertheless Manetho's thirty dynasties are very

OPPOSITE
The principal sites of ancient Egypt

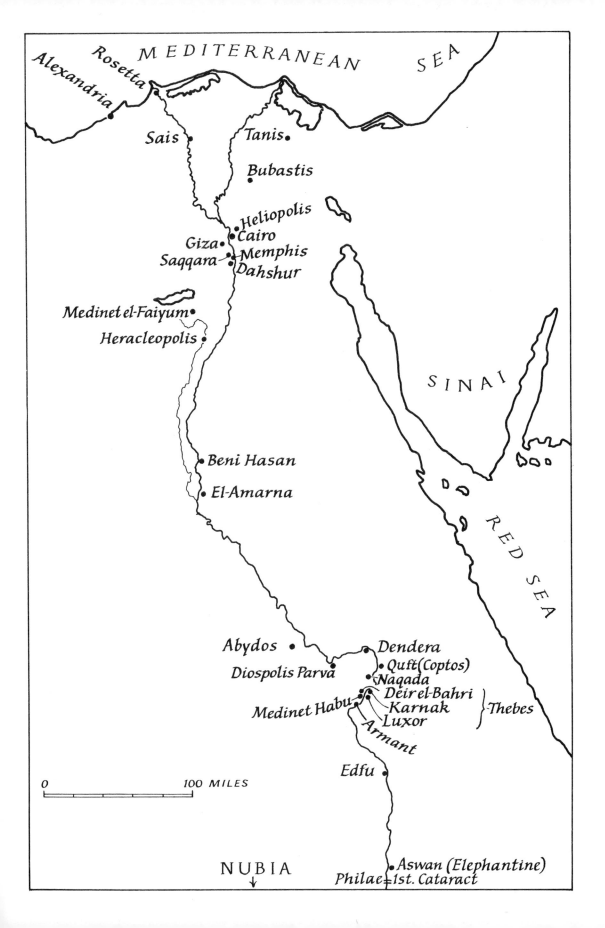

MEDITERRANEAN SEA

Alexandria

Rosetta

Sais

Tanis

Bubastis

Heliopolis
Cairo
Giza
Memphis
Saqqara
Dahshur

Medinet el-Faiyum

Heracleopolis

SINAI

Beni Hasan

El-Amarna

RED SEA

Abydos

Dendera

Diospolis Parva

Quft (Coptos)

Naqada

Deir el-Bahri

Medinet Habu

Karnak

Luxor

Armant

Thebes

Edfu

NUBIA

Aswan (Elephantine)

Philae—1st. Cataract

0   100 MILES

convenient divisions, and they are now firmly established as the framework of any account of Egyptian history.

Any book about ancient Egypt will contain copious references to the most important dynasties, and also to certain periods in Egyptian history when the light of Egyptian civilisation burned brightest. These periods are the Old, Middle and New Kingdoms. How do they fit into the dynastic structure? What, in fact, is the sequence of Egyptian history in very broad outline?

Manetho, as we noticed above, began the First Dynasty with Menes, the king who united the Two Lands, the independent kingdoms of Upper (Southern) and Lower (Northern) Egypt. He chose his beginning with remarkable skill because it was precisely at about this time (3100 BC) that the Egyptians began first to write on wood and stone and other materials. A people who can write and leave records to be read and understood in future ages are truly historical; for history in the strictest sense can be written only about people who write. So Egyptian history may be said to begin with Menes and the First Dynasty. There were, of course, Egyptians living, fighting, organising themselves, and making things, before Menes. But as they did not write they cannot be called historic, but prehistoric, or more particularly, predynastic.

Nothing was known about predynastic Egypt until archaeologists began seriously to investigate ancient sites, looking not just for fine works of art, but for information which would illuminate dark periods of ancient history. Towards the end of the nineteenth century excavators unearthed strange cemeteries and settlements up and down the Nile Valley. It was some time before it was realised that the people who had lived and been buried in these places belonged to periods before Menes had become king. From the remains found in these early sites the archaeologists could see that many characteristics of Egyptian civilisation had developed in predynastic times; but the great advance came with the political unification of Upper and Lower Egypt under Menes. The first two dynasties, known as the Early Dynastic Period, or Archaic Period, were a great formative time when many Egyptian institutions were established; writing then developed; many artistic peculiarities appeared for the first time; the practical arts and crafts flourished, and building on a large scale was first contemplated.

The Early Dynastic Period ended in about 2686 BC, and was followed by the Old Kingdom which covered the Third to the Sixth Dynasties. This was the period of pyramid building, the time

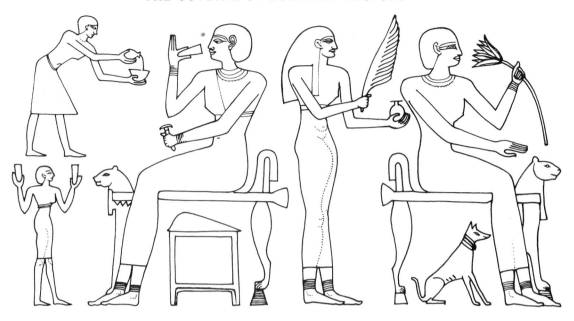

Relief from the lime-stone sarcophagus of Ashait, daughter of King Mentuhotpe II. *On the left* Ashait smells perfume and receives a drink, *on the right* her female attendant fans her. Thebes, *c* 2050 BC.

when the Egyptian king was at his most powerful. He was regarded and treated as a divine person, wholly omnipotent, the centre and hub of the realm. During the Third Dynasty, in the reign of King Zoser, the first great stone building was built—the Step Pyramid—apparently on the inspiration of his chief minister Imhotep. The Great Pyramid, the biggest of all the pyramids, was built by Cheops, the second king of the Fourth Dynasty, as his tomb. In this same dynasty some of the greatest sculptures of Egyptian art were carved. At the same time expeditions began to be sent abroad, chiefly for purposes of trade, not conquest. Egypt had become a strong, centralised, well governed state, wholly able to establish and maintain relations with foreign countries. A relaxation of central control developed in the Fifth and Sixth Dynasties, and the seeds were sown for the collapse of the kingship soon after the reign of Pepi II. He ruled, according to Manetho, for ninety-four years, an exceptionally long reign for ancient Egypt where most people died before they were forty years old.

This collapse came in about 2180 BC, and Egypt relapsed into a condition of anarchy. Local princes assumed control of their petty realms; law and justice disappeared; irrigation, so necessary for the agriculture of the country, was neglected and famine conditions occurred. This calamitous time is now called the First Intermediate Period, and it lasted from the Seventh Dynasty to the Eleventh

Dynasty. Much of what happened during this period is unclear, and Manetho's sequence of dynasties may not properly reflect the succession of power. Gradually two rival groups of principalities or nomes (as the ancient Egyptian provinces are called) developed

Life-size granite statue of King Sesostris III from Deir el-Bahri, *c* 1850 BC.

14

Scene from the tomb of Menna, Thebes, *c* 1420 BC. *Above* tax defaulters are brought before Menna, *below* men working in the fields on the grain harvest.

under the leadership of the two cities of Heracleopolis and Thebes. Out of this struggle Thebes emerged as the victor, and the Theban princes or nomarchs became new uniters of Upper and Lower Egypt. This line of nomarchs formed Manetho's Eleventh Dynasty, and the moment of their triumph came in about 2050 BC.

As kings of the newly reunited Egypt the Eleventh Dynasty rulers ushered in an energetic new period now called the Middle Kingdom. Its greatest brilliance came in the Twelfth Dynasty when kings named Ammenemes and Sesostris brought stability and prosperity to Egypt at home, and fame and respect abroad. The potentially disruptive power of the local princes or nomarchs was broken by the suppression of their offices; their duties were taken over by a well-organised civil service answerable to the king. Egyptian arms won victories in Nubia to the south, and successfully protected Egypt's northern borders from attacks by Asiatics and Libyans. The Middle Kingdom was a period of great cultural activity when many of the classics of Egyptian literature were written, and scientific treatises on medicine, mathematics and other subjects were compiled.

The end of the Middle Kingdom was not marked by such a dramatic breakdown of life in Egypt as was the case with the Old Kingdom. During the Thirteenth Dynasty, which succeeded the Twelfth in about 1786 BC, the traditions and policies of the previous period continued for some time. But the vital force seemed to be lacking, and powerful central government gradually succumbed to hostile influences in the country. The period covered by the Thirteenth to the Seventeenth Dynasties is known as the Second Intermediate Period. As the rule of the legitimate line of Egyptian kings at Thebes became weak, it was strongly challenged by foreign princes who established a rival kingdom in Lower Egypt. These princes were the Hyksos, whom Manetho described as foreign invaders. Recently discovered inscriptions, however, confirm that the Hyksos were the leaders of foreigners who had settled in the Delta of Egypt over a long period of time. They took advantage of the weakening of authority of the Theban kings and set up their own dynasties. The Fifteenth Dynasty of Manetho was made up of the most important Hyksos kings, whose control of Lower Egypt lasted for more than one hundred years. For most of this time Upper Egypt was ruled by native Egyptians from Thebes. They formed the Seventeenth Dynasty and provided an opposition to the Hyksos which gradually increased in strength until active war broke out. Finally, in about 1567 BC, the Hyksos were defeated and driven from Egypt. The victor was the Theban king Amosis who was once more able to assume with justice the royal title 'King of Upper and Lower Egypt'.

Amosis was the first king of the Eighteenth Dynasty and the initiator of the New Kingdom which was to continue for nearly five hundred years until the end of the Twentieth Dynasty in about

Two dancers and four female musicians entertain guests at a banquet provided for the soul of Nebamun. Painting from his tomb at Thebes
c 1400 BC.

1085 BC. This was the period of imperial expansion, when Egypt's power extended far into Asia in the east, and into Nubia in the south. The Egyptian capital at Thebes during the Eighteenth Dynasty was a power-house of activity, a city of great buildings and fine works of art. Life was rich and luxurious for the nobles; in death they hoped to enjoy an equally comfortable existence by way of their beautiful tombs in the vast cemetery across the Nile from Thebes. The kings named Amenophis and Tuthmosis were enlightened despots who were the first rulers of Egypt to adopt as their title the word Pharaoh, which actually means 'Great House' or 'Palace'. Towards the end of the Eighteenth Dynasty came the reign of Akhenaten, the idealistic religious reformer who almost established a religion of one god in Egypt, and, at the same time, almost lost the whole of the Egyptian empire. Tutankhamun, the boy-king, whose tomb was discovered in dramatic circumstances in 1922, reigned just after the death of Akhenaten, in about 1363 BC.

In the Nineteenth and Twentieth Dynasties Egyptian power was vigorously reasserted, especially by the kings Ramesses II and Ramesses III, but strong external pressures from Asiatic tribes constantly threatened the safety of Egypt's empire, and even of the country itself. Ramesses II was the greatest builder of all the Egyptian kings; scarcely an important site lacks the remains of a temple built by him, from the Delta in the north to Abu Simbel in Nubia. A long line of kings, all named Ramesses, brought the Twentieth Dynasty to an end in about 1085 BC. By this time all of Egypt's Asiatic empire was lost, and power in the country was divided between the royal line ruling from the Delta, and the high priests of Amun ruling from Thebes.

The three dynasties numbered Twenty-first to Twenty-third by Manetho, are sometimes called the Late New Kingdom, and sometimes, rather erroneously, the Third Intermediate Period. Throughout this time Egypt lacked strong government, but there was no complete breakdown of life as had happened in the First Intermediate Period. The rulers of the Twenty-second Dynasty were of Libyan stock, but although they were foreigners there seems to have been no positive internal opposition to their rule, probably because they had long been settled in Egypt.

Strength and dignity returned to Egypt with the arrival in about 730 BC of Piankhi, a prince from Napata in Nubia, who conducted a holy crusade to rehabilitate the worship and rule of the Theban

Limestone relief from El-Amarna showing King Akhenaten with his wife Nefertiti and one of their daughters making offerings to the Aten, shown as the sun's disc with rays ending in human hands—the manifestation of sole divinity to Akhenaten

god Amun. He easily conquered the whole country, declared himself King of Upper and Lower Egypt, and established the Twenty-fifth Dynasty. Under Piankhi and his successors a new and vital spirit revivified Egyptian life and culture. The process continued during the Twenty-sixth Dynasty, a line of native Egyptian rulers who achieved power after a short period when the Assyrians under Esarhaddon and Ashurbanipal made raids into Egypt. These new Egyptian kings came from the city of Sais in the Delta, and their rule is usually called the Saite Period. For one hundred years something of the old brilliance of Egypt's ancient civilisation was recaptured. But too many pressures were exerted from outside Egypt for such glory to last.

In 525 BC the Persian king Cambyses invaded Egypt and annexed the land as a satrapy of the Persian Empire. For one hundred and twenty years the Persians ruled Egypt, and their kings were placed by Manetho in the Twenty-seventh Dynasty. After the death of Darius II in 404 BC three native dynasties succeeded in maintaining some sort of Egyptian rule in the face of constant Persian pressure. The last truly Egyptian king, Nectanebos, was finally ousted by Artaxerxes Ochus, the Persian, in 342 BC. This event marked for Manetho the end of his thirty dynasties. Later writers invented a Thirty-first Dynasty to accommodate the Persian rulers who controlled Egypt from 342 BC until 332 BC, when Alexander the Great 'liberated' Egypt from the Persian yoke.

Egypt had by now become a pawn in the game of international power politics. Some time after Alexander's death in 323 BC, a line of Macedonian Greek rulers, the Ptolemies, occupied the Egyptian throne. They did much to promote trade and agriculture, and the country flourished commercially, and indeed culturally, at this time; but all the emphasis was Greek. The last Ptolemaic ruler was the famous Cleopatra, and when she died in 30 BC Egypt was absorbed into the Roman Empire and organised as a Roman province. For three thousand years Egypt had been almost continuously ruled by native kings; almost two thousand years were now to pass before her destiny would once again be controlled by a native Egyptian.

Such then is the bare sequence of Egypt's long history in antiquity. The outline contained in the surviving fragments of Manetho's work still holds good, and the reputation of its author as a trustworthy historian has steadily grown. By itself, however, Manetho's work only provides the barest bones of history. For the rest we must rely on what can be read in the ancient inscriptions, and what can be deduced from material remains. As the years go by, excavation continues and, little by little, new information accumulates. Some new discoveries in themselves provide startling information; others throw light on old discoveries; in the tasks of excavation and interpretation all Egyptologists play their parts.

DYNASTIC CHART

PREDYNASTIC PERIOD	*before* 3100 BC	Progress from primitive society to two kingdoms in Delta and Upper Egypt.
EARLY DYNASTIC PERIOD (Dynasties I, II)	*c.* 3100–*c.* 2686 BC	Unification of Egypt. Great formative period.
OLD KINGDOM (Dynasties III-VI)	*c.* 2686–*c.* 2180 BC	The Pyramid Age. Royal power is supreme.
FIRST INTERMEDIATE PERIOD (Dynasties VII-XI)	*c.* 2180–*c.* 2050 BC	Failure of central control followed by anarchy.
MIDDLE KINGDOM (Dynasties XI, XII)	*c.* 2050–*c.* 1786 BC	Reunification of Egypt by Theban rulers. Great cultural and administrative expansion.
SECOND INTERMEDIATE PERIOD (Dynasties XIII-XVII)	*c.* 1786–*c.* 1567 BC	Return of anarchy. The Hyksos control part of Egypt.
NEW KINGDOM (Dynasties XVIII-XX)	*c.* 1567–*c.* 1085 BC	Expulsion of Hyksos. Egypt's imperial period. Pressures from Asia threaten Egypt.
LATE NEW KINGDOM (Dynasties XXI-XXIII)	*c.* 1085–730 BC	Division of rule between kings in the Delta and priests of Amon-Re at Thebes.
LATE PERIOD (Dynasties XXIV-XXX)	730–332 BC	Egypt subject to invasions by Ethiopians and Assyrians. Revival under Saite kings.
PTOLEMAIC PERIOD	332–30 BC	Conquest of Egypt by Alexander the Great. Rule of Macedonian kings.
ROMAN PERIOD	*after* 30 BC	Egypt absorbed into the Roman Empire.

2

The Beginnings
of Real Archaeology

Visitors to the Great Pyramid at Giza in the winter of 1880–81 might have been surprised to see the strange figure of a man dressed only in pink vest and pants striding purposefully over the rocky plateau, ragged beard blowing about in the wind, fixing surveying posts in the ground and making observations through a theodolite. To dress and behave like this in England at that time would have been considered very bad form, to say the least; but to the man himself what others thought was of little concern. He was busy, and wanted to be as comfortable as possible. If he cut an odd figure and so scared off the curious tourist, it was all to the good. He could then work on undisturbed.

This eccentric behaviour came from a man who was soon to revolutionise excavation in Egypt. William Matthew Flinders Petrie had received an unconventional upbringing and education. His mind was immensely active, his curiosity unbounded, his ingenuity in solving problems unparalleled; his natural instincts were of a scientific kind, but his mental processes, undisciplined by formal training, were erratic and romantically inspired. He came to Egypt first in 1880 at the age of twenty-seven to make the first detailed survey of the pyramids at Giza. He and his father had been much impressed by the writings of Piazzi Smyth, the Scottish Astronomer Royal, who had propounded all kinds of speculative theories based on measurements taken from the Great Pyramid, analysed in terms of a new standard unit which he called the 'Pyramid inch'. Young Flinders Petrie, who had spent much time on archaeological survey at Stonehenge and other southern English prehistoric sites, was determined to establish the truth of Piazzi

Smyth's theories. He came to Giza, measured the monuments, and arrived at a conclusion quite the opposite of what he had set out to prove. It was an important failure for him, and one which he quickly realised contained the germs of success. In archaeology preconceived ideas are almost always dangerous, for the excavator can never be sure of finding what he has set out to find, or of proving what he wants to prove. Dig with hope, but dig with an open mind.

Two seasons surveying the pyramids introduced Petrie to Egypt, and gave him a great desire to continue working there. The book which he wrote about his survey of the pyramids brought him acclaim and a reputation which enabled him to obtain an appointment to excavate for the newly founded Egypt Exploration Fund. So, in 1883 he returned to Egypt and was launched on a career which was to become of the greatest importance to the science of excavation. Up to that time excavation in Egypt had been largely a hunt for museum objects. In the early nineteenth century the rival agents of European collectors and museums squabbled over concessions to dig in the well-known profitable areas like Thebes. Sites were pillaged; no records were kept; precious archaeological information was lost for ever. It is easy now to be harsh on those early 'excavators', but we must remember that there was little realisation at that time of what information could be obtained from properly conducted excavations.

As the century advanced, however, some control was imposed on the wholesale looting of earlier years. In 1858 Auguste Mariette, a Frenchman, was appointed the Conservator of Egyptian Monuments by the Khedive, the ruler of Egypt. His task was to regulate work on ancient sites and to prevent the plundering which had gone on for so long. He himself undertook many excavations, but his methods were not much better than those of the treasure-hunters whose wings he had successfully clipped. He dug to discover inscriptions, interesting structures, and fine objects which would stock the newly founded museum in Cairo. He did not supervise his excavations very well, and did not keep very careful records of his discoveries. He was, like so many who had worked before in Egypt, and indeed were to work there in the future, a scholar who dug, not a true excavator.

Into this undisciplined, rather amateur field stalked the impatient Petrie. From the very beginning of his career in Egypt he behaved like one who had discovered, as if by divine inspiration, what archaeology should really be all about. Nothing he dug up would

Sir Flinders Petrie by de Lazlo. Portrait from the Department of Egyptology, University College London.

be rejected without consideration; every small scrap of ancient material might help to build up the picture of life in remote ages. He himself once wrote: 'I believe the true line lies as much in the careful noting and comparison of small details, as in more wholesale and off-hand clearance.' Consequently, work on a Petrie dig was hard, constant and concentrated. All effort was to be devoted to the work. He was a complete slave to his chosen study, and there

Primitive limestone
figure of the god Min,
c 1100 BC, discovered
by Petrie at Coptos.

could be no room for comfort or luxury. Life at Petrie's camp was
earnest and uncomfortable. The rewards, on the other hand, were
valuable experience and immense stimulation from being in contact
with a fanatic who lived archaeology all his waking hours.

After ten years of excavating in a great many places, mostly in
the Delta and the Faiyum, a fertile depression watered by a side
branch of the Nile, Petrie decided to excavate with a particular aim
in mind. You will remember that as far as Manetho was concerned
the history of Egypt began with the unification of the two lands of
Upper and Lower Egypt by Menes at the beginning of the First
Dynasty. Before Menes the land was supposed to have been ruled
by gods and demi-gods. In Petrie's time the very existence of the
kings of the first two dynasties as enumerated by Manetho was
questioned. This disbelief in Manetho was due to the lack of
evidence—the absence of monuments bearing names which could
be equated with those given by Manetho. Historians were inclined
therefore to treat Manetho's account of the first two dynasties with
considerable caution, though they were prepared to accept that new
evidence might support what Manetho recorded. As for what
happened before the foundation of the First Dynasty, nobody had
much to suggest. Manetho's gods and demi-gods were naturally
unacceptable to good sceptical historians of the late nineteenth
century. But if Egypt was not ruled by demi-gods before Menes
appeared on the scene, what should be put in their place?

As Egyptian civilisation seemed to these sceptical historians to
appear as if from nowhere, it was proposed that some invading race
must have arrived in Egypt just before the establishing of the First
Dynasty. It was this race which must have given Egyptian civilisation its peculiar character. In Petrie's early years in Egypt there was
much speculation about the 'dynastic race'; about its arrival in
Egypt, its land of origin, and the route by which it reached Egypt.
The obvious source of such an invading race was Asia, and particularly the land of Mesopotamia. As for the route, some scholars,
including Petrie, believed that the invaders crossed the Red Sea
and reached Egypt at a point on the coast near the Wadi Hammamat,
a rocky valley which led through the mountains of the Eastern
Desert of Egypt to the Nile Valley near the present-day town of
Quft. Petrie in 1893 thought that the dynastic race came, not from
Asia, but from further south in Africa, from the land which the
Egyptians called Punt, the source of exotic goods like incense and
ivory and giraffes' tails. He felt it was time to make an active

search for signs of the arrival of the dynastic race and therefore applied to excavate at Quft, a place more generally known by its Greek name Coptos.

Excavations in the temple area at Coptos produced a few results which encouraged Petrie to believe that he was on the right track. Three very crude statues of Min, the local god, could not be fitted into the known pattern of Egyptian sculpture, and Petrie assigned them to a time when the conventions of Egyptian sculpture had not been established. Some scholars now believe that Petrie was wrong to date these statues to predynastic times, but there is still much to be said for his opinion. As far as our present story is concerned, the important fact is that Petrie thought he had discovered traces of a settlement earlier than the First Dynasty. The other important consequence of the work at Coptos was that Petrie found that the local workmen employed by him were unusually gifted excavators. They were careful, honest, diligent, and they took a true interest in the work. So in the future Petrie always employed men of Quft, or Quftis as they are always called, in his excavations in Egypt. This practice became a tradition, and even today most excavators in Egypt rely on a nucleus of Quftis to give substance to their work forces.

In the winter of 1893–94 Petrie turned his attention to a district on the west bank of the Nile opposite Quft from which, he had heard, unusual objects had been dug up by casual diggers. The area lay between the villages of Naqada and Ballas; it contained the remains of a temple, a centre of the worship of Seth, the god sometimes identified by the Egyptians with the forces of evil. The great discovery, however, was a vast cemetery containing graves of a kind never previously excavated in Egypt. Almost three thousand graves were excavated in one season by Petrie's newly founded squad of Quftis helped by unskilled local labourers. The burials were simple, in pit graves, the bodies unmummified and placed on their left sides in crouched positions. Grave goods consisted of pottery in large quantities, of types outside the range of Petrie's experience. In addition to pottery there were slate palettes for mixing eye-paint, carved ivories of strange design, flint knives, copper implements, strings of simple beads and other ornaments, vessels of fine workmanship made from all kinds of hard stones, and a few small figures of human beings and animals.

The task of clearing and recording these graves was tackled by Petrie and his chief assistant, James Quibell, with a systematic

A recent excavation in Nubia, south of Abu Simbel. In the foreground stand Qufti workmen who still display the exceptional skills in excavation which were first detected in their forefathers by Flinders Petrie.

attention to detail never previously applied to archaeology in Egypt, and possibly anywhere else. Unskilled boys and men were used to discover the graves, usually indicated by soft patches of gravel, and to begin the clearance. When a grave had been cleared down to the appearance of the first object, skilled men took over. They completed the clearance, leaving every object in the burial in its proper position, and the skeleton cleaned bare of all earth. Petrie or one of his assistants then made a careful drawing of the burial noting all the objects, before everything was removed and numbered. By the end of the season a remarkable record had been built up, out of which in due time one of the most important systems of dating archaeological material was constructed, the system known as 'sequence dating'.

At first Petrie was baffled by his discoveries at Naqada. Where could he place historically the people whose graves he had found? By a series of arguments, which we now know to be wrong, he reached the conclusion that he had found a cemetery of people who lived during the First Intermediate Period, that shadowy time between the Sixth and the Eleventh Dynasties. Unable to be more precise about these people, who seemed so un-Egyptian, he assigned them to what he called the 'New Race'. The problem did not remain unsolved for long. First a French archaeologist, J. de Morgan, and then Petrie himself excavated sites which revealed clearly that the people who were buried with grave goods like those found at Naqada, lived before the First Dynasty. Furthermore, some of the types of Naqada pottery were also found in burials securely dated to the First Dynasty. This pottery therefore demonstrated the continuity between the cultures of the predynastic period and of the First Dynasty.

In the season 1898–99 the site which claimed Petrie's attention lay between Dendera and Abydos, two places which possess fine temples and other important ancient remains. The chosen area was in the neighbourhood of Hu, in ancient times an important provincial centre, known later to the Greeks as Diospolis Parva. Here Petrie found further cemeteries which belonged to the predynastic peoples, and as a result of his work there he was able to consolidate his knowledge of this very early period, and bring order into what seemed a chaotic mass of archaeological material.

To the count of almost three thousand graves at Naqada he was able to add many hundreds more at Diospolis Parva. How could the thousands of pots and other objects from these tombs be organised to produce a sequence by which early, late, and middle-period graves could be dated? Petrie was a great compiler of series. He had a keen eye for significant detail, and realised early in his career as an archaeologist that only by the study of all the different kinds of a particular object could good conclusions be drawn. He was devoted to the idea of the 'corpus'. If you collect together all the different kinds of beer-bottles and properly classify them you can claim to have made a corpus of beer-bottles. If you have a corpus of beer-bottles which is fairly complete you should be able to place within its limits any other beer-bottle of a new kind which may turn up in the future. Applying this idea to archaeological finds, Petrie prepared a corpus of each of the different categories of objects found in the predynastic graves, in the hope that he could roughly arrange them in chronological order.

Pottery vessel of the Naqada II period decorated with paintings of a boat and ostriches.

From his study of the thousands of pottery vessels found at Naqada Petrie had built up a corpus of 700 kinds of pots arranged in nine principal groups. He found that he was able to fit the pots from Diospolis Parva without much difficulty into this corpus. Every grave contained some pots, and so pots were ideally suitable for the preparation of a chronological sequence. Of the nine groups of pots one was particularly distinctive. He called it 'wavy-handled'

The development of
wavy-handled vases.
An illustration of how
Petrie developed his
method of sequence
dating

because the pots had simple handles which in the best examples
were wavy, rather like pieces of crust from the edge of a pie. He
noted that changes took place in the form of these handles, accompanied by changes in the general shapes of the pots. So the various
shapes were placed in a sequence which seemed to correspond
with a line of regular development. Pots of other kinds found along
with particular shapes of wavy-handled vessels could then be tied
into the sequence. Gradually all the pottery was organised in this
way until a great series was compiled. Of course the final series was
not achieved without a great deal of trial and error. It also had to
be tested for general accuracy against the material in the other
corpuses—the stone vessels, the slate palettes, and so on.

When the sequence was complete and well tested, the whole
range was divided into fifty sections numbered from 30 to 80. At
number 30 were placed the earliest pots; at 80 came the latest pots
which could be dated just before the First Dynasty. Each number
between 30 and 80 was called a sequence date. By assigning
sequence dates to newly discovered predynastic material Petrie
could place it within the series. If, for example, he excavated a
grave at some other site, by examining the pottery found in it he
could give sequence dates to each type of pot. One type might occur
between sequence dates 30 and 37; another between 30 and 50;
·another between 31 and 63; and a fourth between 35 and 71. The
only common sequence which would allow for all these types lies
between 35 and 37. So it would be a fair conclusion to date that
grave to sequence dates 35–37.

The series was started at 30 so that any earlier material found in
subsequent excavations could be accommodated at the lower end
of the sequence. Similarly the top end could be continued forward
to cover material of the First Dynasty. However, it was for the
dating of predynastic antiquities that sequence dates were of
greatest importance. As a relative method of dating the system

remained an invaluable tool for decades, and some archaeologists still find it a convenient way of placing objects in the undatable Predynastic Period.

Petrie's work on the predynastic cemeteries at Naqada has become a classic enterprise in Egyptian archaeology. Nowadays the two principal predynastic cultures are usually called Naqada I and Naqada II. But the importance of the Naqada excavation lies not only in the great discoveries made by Petrie, but also in the way he exploited his discoveries to the lasting benefit of archaeologists working in the field and scholars working in their studies. The principles of observation and recording developed by him in his early excavations became the pattern for others to follow. Petrie himself, sadly, was in his late career too often in a hurry to conform strictly to his own principles. He became obsessed with the way in which ancient sites were being plundered and tried to anticipate the plunderers by digging in as many places as possible. In consequence he never spent long enough on any one site to solve the problems raised by his work. But he never dug carelessly, he was always a careful recorder of small detail, and he always published his results promptly. The fact that he is so much criticised by archaeologists today is a measure of the very high standards he himself set at a time when Egyptian archaeology was quite undisciplined.

3

Discovering Pyramids

Zakaria Goneim's chief claim to fame is that he found a pyramid. 'How', you may ask, 'can a pyramid be lost so as to need finding?' The Great Pyramid at Giza after all has a base with sides 755 feet in length, and it stands 450 feet high. The Step Pyramid at Saqqara has sides at its base of between 411 feet and 358 feet, and it stands 204 feet high. The very idea of losing either of these pyramids is ridiculous. Yet the pyramid found by Zakaria Goneim has sides approximately 395 feet long at the base. How could a vast structure like this be so lost that even in a well-trodden place like Saqqara it remained unnoticed until 1952?

The story of the discovery of this hitherto unknown pyramid is one of romance and, ultimately, of tragedy. Saqqara lies about seventeen miles south of Cairo. It is a vast burial area, the cemetery of the great city of Memphis. From the time of the First Dynasty the nobles who attended the king in this first capital of Egypt built their tombs at Saqqara. Perhaps even some of the kings of the First Dynasty were buried there. Later in the Old Kingdom kings did build pyramid-tombs at Saqqara. One pyramid in particular dominates the scene; it is the Step Pyramid, built for Zoser, second king of the Third Dynasty. In his reign Egyptian civilisation reached its first great peak, and the achievements of the time are usually credited to Imhotep, Zoser's chief official. It is impossible to know precisely how responsible Imhotep was for the greatness of Zoser's reign, but he must have been an extraordinary man to have gained such a reputation that it lasted in the memories of men for two thousand years. In late times in Egypt he was so revered that a cult was established at Saqqara and he was worshipped as a god. He was thought of as the completely clever man, endowed with every kind of talent and virtue. Much of his later reputation was undoubtedly built on myth, but there can be little doubt that he had played an important role at Zoser's court and was closely involved in the planning and building of the Step Pyramid.

Nothing like it had ever been seen in Egypt before. To begin with, it was built entirely of stone, whereas most earlier building had been of mud brick. Then it was designed on an unparalleled scale; it seems big to us today, but it must have seemed vast when it was new. It was, furthermore, far more than a tomb alone. The pyramid consisted of six stages set one on top of the other in diminishing size. Beneath it were subterranean chambers and passages designed to receive the burials of the king himself and of members of his family, and great quantities of funerary equipment which the dead would need in the life after death. For the ancient Egyptians believed that after death life would continue beyond the grave in a way very similar to life on earth.

Zoser's great tomb was placed in an enclosure surrounded by a stone wall built of the finest limestone which even today shines brilliantly in the bright sunlight over the desert. It is thought that

Part of the enclosure wall of the unfinished pyramid of Sekhemkhet just after its discovery by Zakaria Goneim.

with this great enclosure Imhotep was creating for the king's after-life a replica of the palace area in Zoser's capital city. Apart from the royal tomb the enclosure contained other buildings which seem to reproduce structures which might have been found at Memphis for the celebration of the king's coronation, for the jubilee which he would celebrate after thirty years on the throne. What Imhotep apparently attempted at Saqqara was to provide the king with a setting in which he could perform his royal functions even in death.

This noble aim and the majestic monument erected to help in its achievement established a new tradition for the building of royal tombs. It also set such a high standard that nothing of its kind precisely was subsequently attempted. At least that was the established opinion of archaeologists until Zakaria Goneim found his pyramid. A member of the Egyptian Antiquities Service, he was appointed Chief Inspector of Antiquities at Saqqara in 1951. Soon after his appointment he decided to excavate an area to the south of the Step Pyramid which had never previously been examined. On the ground it seemed a stretch of desert with few distinctive features, slightly elevated above the surrounding country. It was littered with fragments of worked stone, and here and there were outcrops of rough masonry. On an aerial photograph, however, it seemed clearly to contain the remains of an extensive building. So, with a handful of chosen Qufti workmen Zakaria Goneim began to dig. He had little idea of what he would find.

At first the results were more confusing than illuminating. Great masses of rubble masonry, cross walls, traces of ramps, appeared. Some of the masonry seemed designed to produce a flat terrace on

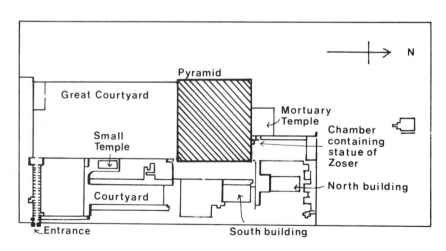

The pyramid complex of Zoser at Saqqara

which further building could take place. Zakaria Goneim suspected that he might have stumbled on an enclosure something like that of Zoser, although it apparently lacked a pyramid. Confirmation of his idea came when a large section of a wall faced with fine white limestone was uncovered towards the north side of the area. In appearance and method of construction it was very similar to the enclosure wall of the Step Pyramid. Zakaria Goneim even found the name Imhotep in red paint in rough hieroglyphs on one block. The quality of the masonry in the new wall was, however, rather inferior to that of the Step Pyramid wall. It gave the impression that a hasty attempt had been made to build a second great funerary monument which had never been carried through to completion.

Work in subsequent seasons confirmed this impression. First the lowest 'step' of a pyramid nearly four hundred feet square was found, together with traces of a second step. The surviving parts nowhere rose to more than about 23 feet above the level of the terrace, and the whole pyramid core had been so overlaid with rubble and sand that it had at first looked like a natural low hill. Then Zakaria discovered a trench on the north side of the pyramid which led to a tunnel. In turn this tunnel led downwards to a chamber directly below the point where the apex of the pyramid would have been. Here lay a fine alabaster coffin spread with withered garlands of flowers, apparently intact. By now, from the mud seals of wine jars found in the subterranean tunnel, the name of the owner of the pyramid had been determined. He was Sekhemkhet, Zoser's successor, otherwise only known from a few sculptured reliefs in Sinai. Was it possible that his mummified body still lay in this coffin?

On June 26 1954 the ceremony of opening the coffin took place. Unlike most stone coffins this one opened not at the top, but at one end where there was a sliding panel. Slowly the panel slid out of place; quickly the hopes of the onlookers were dashed. It was quite empty, and not only empty, but clean as well. Nothing had ever been put inside. How could all this be explained? Was the burial never made and the pyramid never completed? Was this a dummy burial, the real burial chamber having been sited elsewhere? Although Zakaria Goneim worked for one more season and investigated many more subterranean corridors beneath his pyramid, he found little more to encourage him apart from a few pieces of gold jewellery, an ivory tablet with the second name of Sekhemkhet, some stone vessels, and a lot of papyri of a much later period.

Diorite statue of Chephren, builder of the Second Pyramid and the Sphinx at Giza.

33

The alabaster sarcophagus found in the unfinished pyramid of Sekhemkhet. Zakaria Goneim studies the problem of opening the unusual sliding panel at its foot.

Whatever further secrets the partly excavated site might hold, it was not to be Zakaria Goneim who would discover them. In 1959, persecuted by the slanders of jealous colleagues, he was found drowned in the Nile. The empty coffin had been made to appear a symbol of his own personal failure.

The unsatisfactory outcome of Zakaria Goneim's work on Sekhemkhet's pyramid is all too typical of many excavations. Hopes of exciting discoveries are often unfulfilled; expectations are so often frustrated by unexpected developments. It is more than probable that Sekhemkhet's pyramid was never built beyond the second step, and it is even likely that the king may have been buried elsewhere. To embark on the construction of a great tomb was a considerable

34

act of faith on the part of the ruling Egyptian king. Would he live to see it completed and ready to receive his body? It must often have happened that death struck before the tomb was completed. If a burial were made in an unfinished tomb, no further work would be carried out on it after the funeral had taken place, although in the case of a royal burial probably the funerary temple would have been completed sufficiently to allow daily offerings to be made. Archaeologists, however, try to make the most of their discoveries, even if they do not quite come up to expectation. From an unfinished pyramid much can be learned about methods of construction, and Zakaria Goneim's discovery will always have its importance for this reason. In time it may yield other information because new excavations on a limited scale have been resumed on the site in recent years.

The great Step Pyramid of Zoser and the unfinished pyramid of Sekhemkhet were but the first of a long series of great tombs built in pyramid form. Step pyramids were not really pyramids in the strictest sense. When pyramids are spoken about most people think of the three pyramids of Giza, built by kings of the Fourth Dynasty. Their design differs from that of the Step pyramids in that their sides slope gradually. If you go to Giza today and look at the Great Pyramid you will see a vast structure, imposing by any standards, but not quite what it was when it was first built. Then the sides were faced with fine limestone, laid so as to give completely smooth surfaces. This limestone was the best building stone available in the region and when the Arabs came and founded Cairo in the Middle Ages they stripped the Great Pyramid and the other pyramids at Giza of their outer surfaces, and used the stone to build many of the mosques and other public buildings in the new Egyptian capital.

Perfection of design and ease of access have always made the Giza pyramids particular objects of wonder. Herodotus retells many stories about their construction based on what he had been told by his Egyptian guides. He reports, for example, that it took ten years to build the approach causeway to Cheops' pyramid and to prepare the site. A full twenty years were needed for the actual building of the pyramid. Wooden machines were used for the raising of the blocks of stone from level to level, and the whole was finished off with polished blocks fitted together with great accuracy. Armies of men were employed on the construction—he says 100,000 at a time, relieved every three months. His well-informed

The entrance corridor in the Great Pyramid of Cheops at Giza.

guide pointed out a text written on the pyramid which stated the quantities of radishes, onions and garlic consumed on the work. The same guide said that 1600 talents of silver were expended on

these provisions. Herodotus reflects on what the cost of feeding and clothing would have been, and considers the vast amount that was surely spent on providing iron tools for the work.

Two thousand years had already passed between the construction of Cheops' pyramid (the Great Pyramid) and Herodotus' visit. It is not surprising therefore to find in the Greek historian's account some statements which cannot be confirmed by archaeology, and others which can with certainty be challenged. Yet there is more than a grain of truth in what he has to say. The labour force used on the construction cannot now be estimated, although from a knowledge of the size of the stones and of the methods of transport available in the Fourth Dynasty, it is possible to make suggestions about the kinds of gangs used. Most of the stone for the Great Pyramid was quarried locally, so that no great distance was involved in bringing it to the site. The fine limestone for the outer casing however, came from quarries at Tura on the other side of the Nile Valley, about fifteen miles upstream, while the granite used in the burial chamber came all the way from Aswan, five hundred miles to the south. The average weight of the limestone blocks is two and a half tons; the granite blocks are much heavier, the nine slabs forming the ceiling of the royal burial chamber amounting together to about 400 tons.

How were such massive blocks transported? The Nile provides the answer to this question; the Nile was the highway of Egypt. Scarcely anywhere in its course, from the First Cataract at Aswan to the Delta just north of Cairo, is the width of the cultivated Nile Valley more than a dozen miles. A loaded barge could travel all the way from the Aswan quarries to a quay opposite Giza with little difficulty. When the Nile was in flood and the water covered the land between the river and the desert escarpment, a barge could come to within a few hundred yards of the pyramid site. Archaeologists now think that most of the transporting of stone from the quarries to Giza took place during the three months each year, between June and September, when the Nile was in flood. Then would the large quantities of labour be needed, and then indeed would the men be readily available. For during the time of the Nile flood no agricultural work could be done on the land.

Herodotus may have been chiefly responsible for the belief that the pyramids were built by slave labour. Historians now have shown that slavery in the modern, or even the Greek, sense did not exist in Egypt in the remote times of the Fourth Dynasty. No one

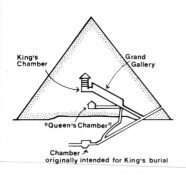

King's
Chamber

Grand
Gallery

"Queen's Chamber"

Chamber
originally intended for King's burial

Cross-section of the
Great Pyramid of
Cheops at Giza

can believe that the Egyptian peasant had much choice when he was recruited to work on royal building projects, but he was not a slave, and would return to his village when the work season ended. The kind of food recorded by Herodotus probably reflects fairly accurately what the workmen ate. Even today the Egyptian workman on an excavation will exist during the day on a diet of bread and onions. In antiquity food and clothing were the equivalent of pay. It is not likely that any formal inscription preserved in detail the quantities of food issued to the builders of the Great Pyramid, but it is possible that some scribbled text contained the information given to Herodotus. Such details were recorded by ancient scribes on limestone flakes, and similar accounts of rations issued to workmen have been found in other places in Egypt.

On the methods of construction used in building the Great Pyramid, Herodotus seems to have been quite misinformed. No archaeologist has ever found any trace of the sorts of machine described for the raising of the blocks. Nowadays it is generally believed that ramps were used on which the stones were dragged to higher levels; sledges and wooden rollers were the only pieces of equipment the Egyptian had at his disposal at that time; the wheel was not yet known to him. The ramp theory has received much confirmation by the discovery of parts of ramps on the site of Zakaria Goneim's unfinished pyramid of Sekhemkhet. As for the iron tools about which Herodotus speculated, it is now known that iron was not available to the Egyptians in any quantity until many centuries after the building of the pyramids. The expedition of Colonel Howard Vyse and J. S. Perring, working on the Great Pyramid in 1837, did find a large piece of iron between two blocks of stone, and for many years it was thought to provide some evidence for the existence of iron tools in the Fourth Dynasty. What had been found, however, was probably part of a tool used by an Arab workman trying to remove stones or to break into the pyramid in medieval times.

In the study of archaeology the material discovered in field-work does not change, but its interpretation often does. The iron found by Vyse and Perring was not the only discovery of theirs which has suffered reinterpretation. In the third and smallest of the big pyramids of Giza they found parts of a wooden coffin and fragments of a human body. Inscriptions on the coffin contained the name of Mycerinus, the king for whom the pyramid had been built. It was a reasonable assumption in 1837 that the coffin was in fact the one provided for the royal burial; presumably the bones were parts of the king's mummy. Both conclusions have subsequently been disproved. From the form of the coffin and the style of the hieroglyphs in the inscription it is certain that it was made in about 600 BC. At that time (the Twenty-sixth Dynasty) much interest was taken in the most ancient monuments in Egypt, and it is known that some pyramids, like the Step Pyramid, were entered and studied by the antiquaries of the day. It is probable that the pyramid of Mycerinus was also entered at this time, the burial found looted, and a new coffin provided for the damaged royal body. But the bones found

A contemporary drawing of the scene in the burial chamber in the pyramid of Mycerinus at the time of its opening by Vyse and Perring. The elaborate sarcophagus was subsequently lost at sea on its way to England.

by Vyse and Perring were equally not the bones of the king. Carbon-14 tests on the remains, carried out in recent years, have shown that the body was about 1500 years old, and therefore was probably that of an intruder who had died inside the pyramid. So do new techniques and new knowledge lead to the modification of what at one time seemed certain fact.

The fascination exercised by the pyramids has led many people over the centuries to interpret them in peculiar ways. Herodotus thought of them as royal monuments, not specifically as tombs, although his guides must have known their true purpose. They have been described as repositories of human knowledge built by divine inspiration; as the granaries built by Joseph to store Pharaoh's grain; as astronomical observatories; and even as constructions embodying in their measurements the predetermined course of history. Scientific investigation of the pyramids has over a period of more than one hundred years built up a solid body of knowledge about them, and yet there are still determined people who are convinced that much remains to be discovered. One large and expensive operation recently launched has aimed at discovering by a form of X-ray process whether the pyramids contain undiscovered chambers.

No one can rule out the possibility of further discoveries, but a consideration of the purpose of a pyramid should cool down excessive expectation. Egyptologists are wholly agreed that a pyramid is a tomb. Excavations have shown that it is part of a collection of structures which together make up a royal funerary monument. The typical complex consists of two temples, linked by a causeway, and the pyramid. One temple, the so-called Valley Temple, stands at the edge of the desert escarpment just above the plain of the Nile Valley. It was a place of reception where the body of the dead king was brought before it was finally carried to the pyramid for burial. By then the body had undergone a long process of dehydration and treatment with purifying salts, ointments, oils, and herbs, by which it was hoped to preserve it for all eternity. This process took seventy days and involved the removal of the brain from the head and the internal organs (except for the heart) from the body. Lastly the treated body was wrapped in bandages and sheets of linen and became what is called a mummy. From the Valley Temple the mummified body was taken up the causeway to the second temple, the Mortuary Temple, which usually lay close to the east side of the pyramid itself. In this temple the regular mortuary services for the dead king were conducted in the years following the burial. In the pyramid was the burial chamber where the royal body was laid to rest. From there the divine royal spirit ascended to join the sun-god in the heavens, perhaps assisted in his ascent by the very form of the pyramid which pointed upwards to the heavens.

The three pyramids at Giza had all been entered long before any modern archaeologist investigated them. They were probably first violated and robbed in remote antiquity. But throughout the ages the myth has persisted that they contain treasures, and many attempts have been made to discover their precious contents. When Colonel Vyse and Mr. Perring went to Giza in 1837, their aim was to make a scientific investigation of the site as far as was possible in those early days of archaeology. Their results are still of importance for pyramid studies, as are those of Flinders Petrie, whose work at Giza introduced him to Egyptology. Since the First World War excavation at Giza has concentrated more on the areas of tombs lying around and between the pyramids than on the pyramids themselves; one of the startling discoveries of this time is described in the next chapter. But the pyramids continue to exercise an extraordinary fascination on succeeding generations. The prosaic explanations of scholars do little to quench irrational enthusiasms, and there can be little doubt that in a thousand years hence some men will still be seeking to unravel the mysteries they believe to be locked in these great structures. Others perhaps will hope to find treasures in undiscovered chambers. Such is the urge to discover something new about the pyramids that all the reasonable arguments of scholars will not persuade the enthusiasts to abandon their hopes.

4

A Triumph of Painstaking Archaeology

'The King is a god and omnipotent,' is the message proclaimed by the pyramids of Giza. The Great Pyramid in particular demonstrates the power of King Cheops, its builder. Yet his achievement was not unique or wholly new. His father, Sneferu, had built two pyramids for himself at a place called Dahshur, about fifteen miles to the south of Giza, and both were very big, though not quite as big as Cheops' pyramid. In the neighbourhood of Sneferu's pyramids, some of the most important nobles of his time built their own tombs. To be buried near the sepulchre of the royal master would enable the dead to participate in some way in the advantages of the royal after-life.

This practice, which had not been wholly unknown in earlier times, was carried to an extreme under Cheops and his successors at Giza. The king, all-powerful in life, would need service and homage in the life to come. So it was arranged that the nobles and high officials who served the king in life should be buried in cemeteries surrounding the royal pyramid. Their tombs were laid out in neat rows or streets; each had a visible part above ground, shaped like a bench and usually called a *mastaba* (the Arabic word for 'bench'); below ground was the burial chamber at the bottom of a deep shaft. There is no evidence that the nobles were put to death when the king died, although this fate may have overtaken their predecessors in earlier times.

Presumably, as each noble died, he took up posthumous occupation of his tomb which was already prepared. No doubt the dead king might have long to wait before his court in the after-life was complete. In death the nobles were not allowed in any way to

The Pyramid of Chephren at Giza, its casing still in position at the apex, with the Great Sphinx in the foreground.

43

diminish the glory of their sovereign, and so their tombs were very plain. The *mastaba* above ground contained a small chapel or offering niche where food and drink for the dead man could be placed. In this chapel a slab was set up carved with a scene in which the owner of the tomb was shown receiving the offerings needed for his survival after death. These slabs, or funerary stelae, as they are usually called, have in many cases survived to modern times, and they tell us precisely who was buried in particular tombs. The burial chamber below ground beneath the chapel was reached by a shaft; it contained the body, and possibly a small amount of personal equipment for use in the after-life. Frequently a head made of limestone, representing the dead noble, was placed near the burial, to take the place of the actual head of the tomb's owner if that were ever damaged. Whoever introduced the idea of the 'reserve head' was a man of shrewd and prudent judgement. For after a tomb had been entered by plunderers, probably in antiquity, and stripped of its valuable and useful contents, practically the only thing left untouched was the 'reserve head', because it was of no value to the

The pyramid area at Giza

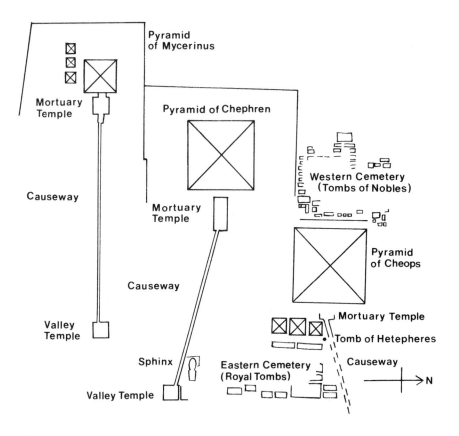

Pyramid of Mycerinus

Mortuary Temple

Pyramid of Chephren

Western Cemetery (Tombs of Nobles)

Causeway

Mortuary Temple

Pyramid of Cheops

Causeway

Mortuary Temple

Valley Temple

Tomb of Hetepheres

Sphinx

Eastern Cemetery (Royal Tombs)

Causeway

N

Valley Temple

Surface view of the tomb discovered by Reisner's expedition in February 1925.

robbers. So it could continue, magically, to consume the offerings symbolically presented to the dead man on his offering stela.

The robbing of so many important tombs has denied us the possibility of building up a good picture of the daily life of Egyptians in the Fourth Dynasty. Furthermore, we should not know much about the skill and artistry of the craftsmen of the period but for an unexpected discovery made on an excavation conducted by the American Egyptologist, George Andrew Reisner. Since 1902 he had been working at Giza, first for the University of California, and later for Harvard University and the Boston Museum of Fine Arts. Reisner was a remarkable man, and as an excavator he

45

employed methods far in advance of his time. Nothing was too unimportant to be overlooked; every detail had to be written down; no object should be moved before it was photographed in position, and drawn. His field-notes were so careful and so complete that scholars who had never visited his excavations were able to write the published reports many years after Reisner's death. His energy was immense, his enthusiasm boundless; he excavated in many sites in the course of single seasons, amassing vast quantities of information and discovering many beautiful objects. But there is no doubt that his most important excavations were those at Giza.

When an excavator undertakes work in Egypt he is granted by the Egyptian Antiquities Service a concession covering a clearly defined area within which he has sole rights to dig. Reisner's concession at Giza lay to the west of the Great Pyramid, the area of the pyramid of Mycerinus, and the space between the east side of the Great Pyramid and the Sphinx. He began work by digging a great many *mastaba* tombs in the first part of his concession, and then in 1924 he turned to the east cemetery. None of the tombs he had excavated contained much in the way of objects. This was hardly surprising because the nature of these tombs was such that they offered little difficulty to the determined tomb robber. Each tomb was marked by its characteristic, rectangular, bench-like superstructure which concealed the top of the shaft leading down

The sight which greeted the eyes of the excavators when they opened the tomb.

to the burial chamber. This shaft was regularly in the same position in relation to the superstructure, so that it was not difficult for plunderers to find it and to dig down to the chamber containing the desirable grave goods.

Knowing how easy it was for such tombs to be identified, entered and robbed, Reisner had few hopes of discovering more than fragments of objects and, perhaps, pieces of sculpture in the *mastabas* he excavated. But the job was worth doing because there was still much to be learned about the burial practices of the Fourth Dynasty. And there was always the chance that something unexpected might turn up.

The season's work began on November 1 1924. At the start much general clearance and survey was carried out. Nothing of striking importance was discovered. Then on February 9 1925 the expedition photographer when setting up his tripod noticed an unusual patch of plaster on the cleared surface of the ground. At first this patch was just noted, and it was only several days later that it was carefully recorded and removed. A cutting filled with small, carefully trimmed, limestone blocks was uncovered. As the blocks were removed, a short stair of twelve rock-cut steps was revealed, leading down to a shaft which ran upwards as well as downwards. The upper end of the shaft was cunningly concealed by rough boulders so carefully placed that they looked like part of the ground surface. No superstructure seemed ever to have covered the shaft.

Like the cutting, the shaft was filled with blocks of limestone set in plaster. Every indication pointed to the probability that whatever lay at the bottom had remained undisturbed since the shaft was filled. Excitement mounted as the layers of stone were removed. At about thirty feet down a small niche was discovered containing the remains of a sacrifice of haunches of oxen and jars of beer. At forty feet there were fragments of a pottery basin; at fifty-six feet, pieces of copper; at seventy-two feet, fragments of a pottery bowl. Below, the layers of stone contained many pottery fragments, and then at eighty feet the eager workmen reached a course of very carefully laid masonry. When this, and the layer below, had been removed the line of the roof of a side chamber could be seen. On the evening of that day, March 7, one block in the wall filling was removed by Mr. Alan Rowe, Reisner's assistant, and in the poor light he could just make out a stone coffin and the glitter of gold. He replaced the block and waited for the following

OPPOSITE
Above Vignette from
the Great Harris
Papyrus showing King
Ramesses III before
the three gods of
Thebes, Amon-Re,
Mut and Khons,
c 1160 BC.
Below Wooden fishing
and fowling skiff. One
of the wooden models
from the tomb of
Meketre, *c* 2000 BC.

day to dawn. Expectation had mounted day by day as the shaft had been cleared; it would not do now to rush the opening of the chamber.

On the following day part of the entrance blocking was again removed and the excavators could at last observe what they had found. To help them see, they mounted a large mirror at the top of the shaft and directed the sunlight to the bottom where it was deflected into the chamber by a disc covered with silver paper. At one side of the burial chamber stood a fine rectangular alabaster coffin on which lay gold-covered poles and beams which apparently belonged to a canopy of some kind. Other poles had fallen into the space between the coffin and the wall. On one end of the lid of the coffin were several sheets of gold ornamented with inlaid designs made up of small pieces of brightly coloured faience, a kind of glazed material much used by the ancient Egyptians for decoration. The floor was covered with a mass of broken objects, parts of gold-covered furniture, copper and stone vessels, great quantities of pottery, and, everywhere, fragments of gold from unidentifiable objects. This jumble of material lay in a roughly cut chamber about fifteen feet deep, eight feet wide, and six feet high. The floor was completely covered with the debris of what had been an impressive collection of funerary equipment. There was no chance of entering the chamber while it was in this state, so the excavators again exercised their self-control, took some photographs, and, after a few days, blocked up the entrance again and filled up part of the shaft. They realised that a long, laborious task of careful clearance lay before them. Adequate preparations needed to be made for the treatment of the shattered objects when they were removed bit by bit. Furthermore, Reisner, the director of the excavation, was in America, and he would have to assess the situation before the actual task of clearance could begin.

Reconstructed
figure of Queen
Hetepheres from an
inlaid box in her tomb

At Giza plenty of time was allowed for consideration and assessment. Before the tomb was reopened special buildings were prepared for the reception of the objects, and new equipment was assembled for the difficult job of raising delicate things up a shaft nearly one hundred feet deep. As for the nature of the find, Reisner was able to conclude that the chamber contained no ordinary burial, because the shaft was not covered by a *mastaba* superstructure. It was possibly a secret burial, or the reburial of a body moved from some other place. Who it was, was unknown. From the gold it might be thought that it was a royal burial; but

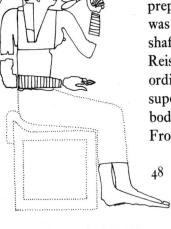

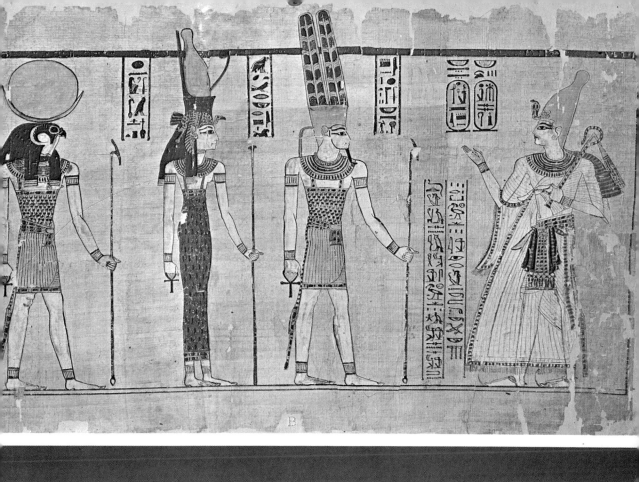

Reisner did not think that it contained a king because the equipment did not seem grand enough. One valuable clue was provided by the inlaid faience designs on the gold sheets. When the tomb was first opened, an Egyptologist using a pair of binoculars was able to read the name of Sneferu, the father of Cheops.

One of Hetepheres' silver bracelets decorated with butterflies inlaid with semi-precious stones

Not until the following February was Reisner ready to start the clearance of the tomb. The whole chamber was in chaos, but, as it was the only tomb of this period to have been found, apparently undisturbed, it was an overwhelming duty of the archaeologists to make sure that every bit of evidence was recovered. It soon became clear that the disarray was caused by the disintegration of the wooden frames of gold-covered furniture. Scarcely anything was known of the furniture of the period, so everything would have to be taken slowly, and knowledge gained as progress was made.

They began with a square foot of floor near the door. Photographs were taken, drawings made, and the top layer of objects removed. The same procedure was followed for the next layer, and so on until the bare floor was reached. Reisner wanted a full record of everything so that in reconstructing the contents of the tomb the relationships of every smallest piece would be clear to anyone working on the material in the future. Slowly the clearance advanced, and the work continued over two long and tedious seasons. Over one thousand photographs were taken and seventeen hundred pages of notes written. And while all this careful grubbing went on, the painstaking tasks of reassembly and study continued above ground.

Gradually the principal facts became clear. The burial belonged to Queen Hetepheres, the wife of Sneferu and the mother of Cheops. Apart from the coffin—which had not yet been opened—the most important items in the funerary equipment were the canopy, a bed, a carrying-chair, two armchairs, a box for the curtains of the canopy, and a jewel box; there were gold vessels and gold cosmetic implements, and silver bracelets. The furniture had been made of ebony and richly overlaid with gold sheet. Some pieces were also inlaid with designs in faience, and some bore inscriptions naming the queen and her royal husband. So carefully was the work of recovery carried out, and so successfully the study of the fragments, that it proved possible subsequently to restore all the chief pieces of furniture, placing the gold coverings on reconstructed wooden cores.

The mystery of the tomb, however, still remained unsolved.

Scene from the tomb of Sennefer at Thebes, showing the tomb-owner and his wife receiving offerings, c 1430 BC.

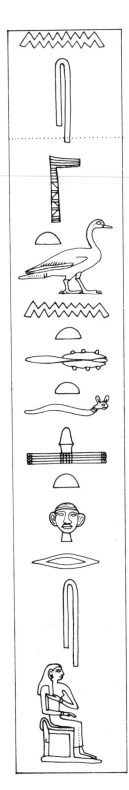

Why was it so secret and, in a sense, so mean? In the slow clearance of the chamber much had been found in the way of unique and beautiful objects. The few inscriptions on the furniture left no doubt that Queen Hetepheres was the person for whom the equipment had been prepared. So much had been found, and yet so few questions had been answered to the satisfaction of the excavators. When all the objects had been removed from the chamber, the alabaster coffin remained. Coffins always induce feelings of respect and reluctance in imaginative excavators—respect for the privacy of the dead, and reluctance to disturb the body. Moreover, opening a coffin is a solemn act. It is also an act full of expectation. What will be inside? In the case of Reisner's excavation it was a fair assumption that Queen Hetepheres would be inside. No one had ever seen a royal mummy of the Old Kingdom.

On March 3 1927, in the presence of a small but distinguished company of visitors, the lid was slowly raised. To everyone's surprise the coffin was empty; a few stains indicated that it had once held something; but there was nothing else. Here was yet another problem to solve. Where was the body? What had happened to it? So the mystery deepened. Then came the last discovery in this strange tomb. In one wall of the chamber there was a niche, closely sealed with plaster and blocks of stone. When they were removed a small alabaster chest was found. Inside it was divided into four compartments which held the remains of the internal organs of Hetepheres. Some of the liquid of the embalming process still remained, unevaporated, in two of the compartments. Removal of the internal organs of a dead person was an essential part of the making of a mummy in later times. Here Reisner discovered the earliest example of its practice. The finding of this chest also proved that there had been at some time a proper burial of Hetepheres. What had happened to her mummy?

The mystery has never been properly solved, but Reisner and his assistants suggested, very plausibly, what may have occurred. Hetepheres, as Sneferu's wife, was probably buried first in a specially constructed tomb at Dahshur, near her husband's pyramids. Some time later, when Cheops was king, robbers entered her tomb, prized open the coffin and removed the mummy. Taking it from the tomb they stripped it of its jewellery, and left the remains to be carried off by jackals. They were probably disturbed in their work before they could complete the robbing of the tomb. When the theft was discovered and reported to the highest officials of the

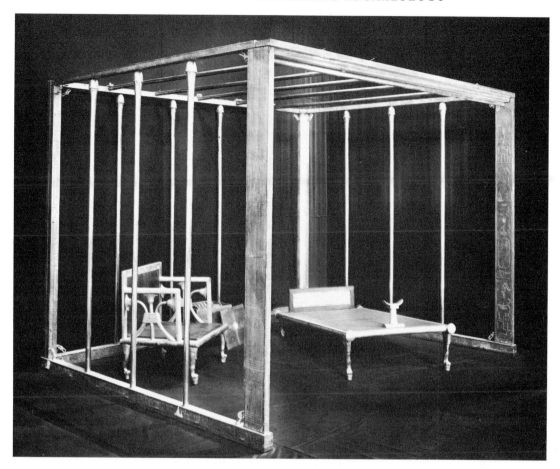

The bed canopy, bed, chair and other items from the tomb of Hetepheres after reconstruction.

OPPOSITE
Part of an inscription from the back of the carrying chair of Hetepheres. The individual signs are of gold and give the queen's name and royal relationship

land, they felt it necessary to conceal the full horror of what had happened from Cheops, but at the same time considered it essential to repair the sacrilege in some way. They therefore told Cheops of the robbery, but did not mention the desecration of the body. Reisner thought that they probably suggested the reburial at Giza where security was greater, and where Hetepheres could eventually participate in the lavish mortuary offerings of her son, Cheops. A makeshift burial chamber was prepared and the empty coffin of Hetepheres, the chest with her internal organs, and the surviving furniture of her first burial were placed within. The shaft was blocked solid and the upper end concealed. Thus, according to Reisner, was the scandal covered up. No doubt some high officers of state breathed more freely when the last blocks of limestone were in position. They would have been even more relieved had they known that 4500 years were to pass before the bodiless burial of Queen Hetepheres would reveal its sacrilegious secret.

51

5

A Great Man
and his Estate

The most important archaeological site in Egypt is Thebes. It lies
four hundred miles up the Nile from Cairo, marked today by the
town of Luxor. The place first became important towards the end
of the First Intermediate Period; it provided the princes who
became the kings of the Eleventh Dynasty and, subsequently, the
upstart family which formed the Twelfth Dynasty. As the place of
origin of the ruling house during the Middle Kingdom, Thebes
achieved dignity, but not the trappings of a royal capital. Not until
the Eighteenth Dynasty did Thebes gain the outer appearance of a
great and important city. From then until Roman times—for
fifteen hundred years—it was among the greatest cities of Egypt,
and for long periods beyond doubt the centre of the Egyptian
world. Its importance was perhaps always derived more from its
religious sanctuaries than from its administrative institutions. The
great temple at Karnak formed a city in itself. Its principal god was
Amon-Re, the divine embodiment of Egyptian imperial power in
the New Kingdom. The temple buildings were vast, and the
power of its priesthood was at times capable of challenging the
authority of the king himself. Thebes was also the place where
important Egyptians from the king downwards chose to be buried,
especially during the New Kingdom.

When an Egyptian died, he journeyed to the 'beautiful west', to
the land where the sun set, and ultimately to the realm of the god
Osiris. So ideally Egyptians were buried on the west side of the
Nile towards the mountains of the Western Desert. At Thebes
therefore the great necropolis or city of the dead lay across the
Nile from Karnak. In addition to tombs there were many temples

in the necropolis area. You will remember that the pyramids had temples attached to them in which the regular royal mortuary services could be performed. In the New Kingdom the kings were not buried in pyramids but in tombs cut deep in the rock of the Valley of the Kings. There was no room for buildings of any size in the Valley of the Kings, so the royal mortuary temples were constructed some distance away.

Of these temples the most striking is that of Hatshepsut, a queen who succeeded in ruling Egypt as if she were a king for about twenty years (1503–1482 BC). Abandoning the usual plan

Deir el-Bahri. Beyond the terraces of Hatshepsut's temple can be seen the temple of Mentuhotpe II.

for such temples, her architects constructed a succession of broad terraces leading to the holy sanctuary. For the site they chose a great bay in the limestone cliffs at a place now called Deir el-Bahri, which in Arabic means 'Northern Monastery', named after a small monastery built in the same place in early Christian times. People who visit Hatshepsut's temple for the first time see the colonnades of the terraces and think that they look rather Greek. For this reason alone the temple had become famous in architectural history. But Greek it certainly is not, as closer inspection soon reveals. And what visitors do not notice, unless their attention is particularly drawn to it, is another temple just to the south, which is also well placed in a bay in the cliffs.

This second temple at Deir el-Bahri was built for King Nebhepetre Mentuhotpe II who was responsible for the reunification of Upper and Lower Egypt at the end of the First Intermediate Period in about 2050 BC. Beneath the temple floor was his tomb, and in the rocky hillside round about were the tombs of his high officials and their successors of the Eleventh Dynasty. Theirs were among the first tombs of any consequence to be built in the Theban necropolis and a fine and dramatic site had been selected, overlooking the temple of Mentuhotpe, with a splendid view eastwards to the green Nile Valley.

Ever since Europeans became interested in Egypt, Deir el-Bahri attracted attention. The prime attraction was the temple of Hatshepsut. Auguste Mariette carried out the first systematic examination of this temple in the mid-nineteenth century, and he was shortly followed by Lord Dufferin, a talented amateur who worked principally on a corner of the Mentuhotpe temple. From 1893 to 1907 Edouard Naville, a Swiss Egyptologist working for the Egypt Exploration Fund, conducted extensive excavations in both temples and in their neighbourhood. In his publication of Mentuhotpe's temple he was rash enough to declare, 'This has been the last campaign, and there will be no more at Deir el-Bahari, since we may now say that Deir el-Bahari is finished.'

How often has an excavator thought that he has completed a site, and how often has he been proved wrong! From 1907 to the present day others have gone to Deir el-Bahri, and still new things are being found there. Since the Second World War a new temple has been discovered. After the First World War a whole series of wonderful discoveries were made by an expedition organised by the Metropolitan Museum of Art, New York.

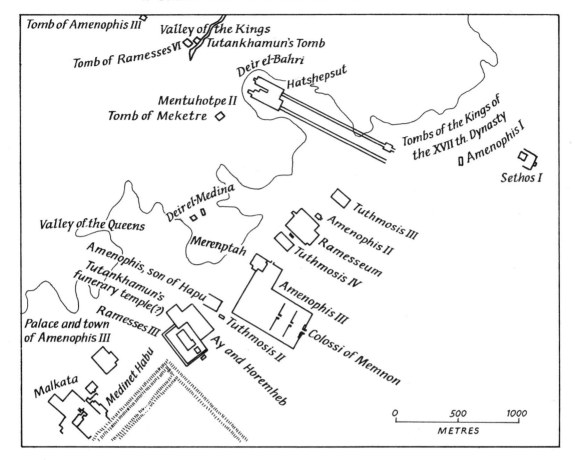

The necropolis area on the west bank of the Nile at Thebes, showing the most important tombs and funerary temples

In the winter of 1919–20 work resumed under the direction of H. E. Winlock, a gifted archaeologist with several years of pre-war experience behind him. Winlock was a very different excavator from Reisner. He possessed flair for discovery, and imagination stimulated by a lively historical sense. He lacked Reisner's incredibly systematic determination, while his attitude towards the purpose of his work was less computerised—if a modern idea may be used to help the comparison. Where Reisner would have welcomed the computer as a valuable tool in archaeology, Winlock, it may be supposed, would have considered it too inhuman. He sought always to illuminate the past, to make the ancients live; and to this end he clothed the bare bones of his discoveries with the trappings of imaginative interpretation.

By some strange fate archaeologists often seem to find the things which suit their manner of working best. Reisner consistently found material that could be card-indexed, organised, submitted

55

to statistical analysis. Winlock found material which clarified the past, throwing light on dark areas, often unexpectedly adding to or filling out previous knowledge.

In 1920 he decided to conduct further investigations into a large, open, rock-cut tomb at Deir el-Bahri, one which had been looked at and apparently cleared twice in 1895 and 1902. It was situated in the cliff face a little way to the south of the Mentuhotpe temple, overlooking another unfinished funerary temple, probably begun for Nebhepetre Mentuhotpe's successor, Sankhkare, also called Mentuhotpe. A broad avenue or ramp led from the valley floor up to the tomb entrance. This avenue was bounded by brick walls, and at the top was a portico of nine columns forming a dramatic façade for the tomb. In the centre of the portico a large doorway gave access to a corridor which stretched twenty yards into the rock, reaching a chapel in which the offerings to the tomb-owner were made. A shaft descended from the floor of the chapel to the burial chamber. A second corridor, chapel and burial chamber had been cut parallel to the main series of rooms, and the two series were linked by a short passage running between the two chapels. It seemed that the second series had been prepared for a relative, probably a son, of the owner of the main tomb.

Much debris still blocked parts of the tomb, but Winlock did not think that much time would be needed to clear it. A little excavation in the court in front of the tomb's entrance produced a fragment of fine relief. It promised that more might be found; its quality showed that the tomb must have been made for a very important person. To start working on a tomb which had already been examined involved a considerable act of faith. But at the beginning Winlock's chief intention was simply to produce a good plan of the tomb. Nothing of the kind had been prepared by the earlier excavators, and as the site lay within the compass of the concession of the Metropolitan Museum, it was something of a duty to make a record even of an apparently worked-out tomb.

As work proceeded further fragments of relief were found, but none was of any size. In that part of the Theban necropolis the rock was of poor quality and the natural walls of the tomb were unsuitable for carving. So they had been faced with high quality limestone brought from elsewhere. At some later date, but probably still in antiquity, this fine stone had been stripped away, no doubt to be used in some other building. The fragments left behind could only hint at the splendour of the original decoration of the

The first view into the chamber beneath the tomb's entrance corridor.

tomb. In the burial chamber likewise, Winlock found only tiny pieces of the owner's coffin, gilded inside and outside.

For several weeks the work continued; it was more like labouring than excavating, for very little was found and very little expected. At last, in the middle of March 1920, it looked as if enough had been done to enable a reliable plan of the tomb to be made. On Wednesday March 17, at the end of the day's work, Winlock was riding his donkey home to the expedition's house down the valley from Deir el-Bahri, when a workman gave him a mysterious message requiring him to return to the tomb. With other members of his staff he hurried back, taking torches as requested. In the corridor they found an excited group of workmen and Harry Burton, the expedition's photographer, waiting with anticipation. They explained that towards the end of the afternoon one of the workmen clearing rubble from the corridor noticed that dust and small stone chippings kept trickling into a crack in the floor. The crack had been enlarged and it became clear that there was a

57

chamber of some kind below. What could it be? Certainly not the tomb's burial chamber, for that was already known. Possibly it was a later burial, dug many years after the original tomb had been robbed and left open. Such intrusive burials, as they are called, are very common, and they are nearly always very mean and dull.

With the crack further enlarged, Winlock went down on his hands and knees and peered in, using one of the flashlights they had brought. What he saw amazed him; it was like looking into a long abandoned toy-cupboard. All kinds of painted wooden models were to be seen, lying about in considerable confusion. There were figures of servant girls engaged in all kinds of activities, domestic animals, several boats, one at least of which had a raised sail. It was impossible to proceed with the examination that evening, so the crack was blocked up, sealed with tapes and sealing wax, and a guard of trusted workmen left to watch over the unexpected discovery. Next day, after preparation of every kind had been made to deal with objects the nature of which was still largely unknown, the work began. At every stage Burton took photographs, using a technique like that employed at Giza to photograph the tomb of Hetepheres. The bright sunlight was deflected by mirrors down the corridor of the tomb, and then reflected by a silverpaper-covered board on to the area to be photographed. So long as the sun shone work could progress.

In front of the crack in the floor of the corridor the top of a short shaft was found, and this turned out to be the entrance to the underground chamber. The shaft was about four feet square, and about the same in depth. It led to a roughly cut chamber about twelve feet square and between four and five feet high. From this

Meketre inspects his cattle.

Meketre and his son
Intef

tiny space the excavators brought out twenty-four wooden models in a variety of kinds and a state of preservation never before equalled. The job of recording the contents and removing them was arduous and dangerous, but not to be compared with the difficulty of excavating Hetepheres' tomb. At Thebes the wood was in good condition; nothing was badly broken; the few detached objects could be recorded in their find places, and later put back in their proper places. Yet haste too was needed because there were constant falls of stone. In three days of unceasing labour the whole clearance was completed, and the excavators could sit back and contemplate what they had obtained.

Models had often been found in tombs of the period from the late Old Kingdom to the early Middle Kingdom (2300–1900 BC). They were usually rough pieces of work, crudely carved and roughly put together. They served as an economical way of providing a burial with scenes of daily activities which might assist a dead person in his existence after death. Never had such models been found as those which were extracted from the anonymous tomb at Deir el-Bahri. And now indeed the tomb ceased to be anonymous, for several of the models included inscribed figures of a man who was clearly the tomb-owner. His name was Meketre and he was chancellor of the king. He was already known from monuments elsewhere, and identified as an official who had begun his career under Nebhepetre Mentuhotpe II and had continued in office under Sankhkare Mentuhotpe III. He probably died while Sankhkare was still on the throne, and he was succeeded in office by his son Intef for whom, it emerged, the parallel tomb had been prepared. Meketre may have been the most powerful royal official of his time; it could at last be understood why the tomb had been so grand, and why it had occupied such a choice site overlooking what was possibly Sankhkare's funerary monument.

From Meketre's models much can be learned about the life of a great noble who lived four thousand years ago. The life illustrated is more domestic than official, for the domestic side of existence was the one to be expected after death. It is Meketre's life on his estates, the life of the great landowner that is shown. Two models represent in summary fashion his house. There behind a high wall lies a garden furnished with trees and a pool—a pleasant place in which to sit during the heat of the day. At one end of the garden is the suggestion of the house: a portico with gaily painted pillars in the form of papyrus and lotus bundles, windows with slatted

59

shutters to keep out the sunlight, a flat roof with water spouts so extended that any rain would be directed into the garden pool.

Seven models illustrate activities on Meketre's estates which may be considered important for the continuation of his life beyond the grave. In the survival of the individual after death the provision of necessary offerings was absolutely essential. Food, drink, clothing were the basic necessities. They might be offered to the spirit of the dead for many years after his burial, for the wealthy man took care to set up a foundation which would ensure the regular presentation of offerings at his tomb. But no Egyptian contemplating the ruins of the past and the desecrated tombs of his ancestors could believe that regular offerings would truly be maintained for himself to eternity, as he desired. So a substitute method was needed. From time to time the method changed. In the days of Meketre something could be done through the scenes on the walls of one's tomb. Further insurance could be made through models.

Among important food offerings were joints of meat, usually taken from prime cattle. Three models are concerned with these offerings. One, the largest model in the collection, shows Meketre's herd being driven before the great man who sits with his son and his scribes and retainers under an awning. An inspection of the herd is taking place, probably to see that all is well with the animals which are intended for Meketre's funerary offerings. A second model represents the cattle shed; some beasts feed quietly in their stalls; others are forcibly fed by the herdsmen to bring them up to the required size for slaughtering. The third model is devoted to that very activity. Two beasts with legs trussed lie on the ground about to have their throats cut; men squat with basins to catch the blood. Bowls of blood heat on fires nearby, a servant plucks a duck, and many joints of meat hang from the roof. Plenty has been prepared for Meketre, and more will be prepared for the future.

If meat was important for a well-balanced diet in the after-life, the two items which were absolutely vital were bread and beer. Both were made from grain, so one model shows Meketre's granary where barley was received from the fields, checked in by the scribes, and stored by warehousemen. In the model devoted to beer- and bread-making the activity is lively and varied. In one section brewing takes place. Dough with yeast in it is prepared, then mixed with water to make a mash which is allowed to ferment. After fermentation the mash is strained and the beer poured into jars. This kind of beer had to be made almost daily, because it had

One of Meketre's
serving women

The carpenter's shop on Meketre's estate.

no powers of lasting. In the other half of the model all the stages of making bread are shown from the grinding of grain to the baking of loaves in primitive ovens. A basket with freshly baked loaves stands ready to be taken to Meketre, along with the jugs of beer waiting in the brewery.

Two more models demonstrated crafts which were important in burial. One shows a weaving shop where two looms are being used to produce lengths of linen cloth. Huge quantities of linen were included in rich burials, and much was needed for the wrapping of mummies. In Meketre's model every step in the preparation of the linen yarn is illustrated. Throughout, women are used for spinning and weaving. Men, on the other hand, dominate the work shown in the other model. Here a carpenter's shop is represented with eleven model craftsmen at work. Some dress timbers, others use saws and chisels, others work at a forge, apparently tempering copper tools. A chest on the floor contains a complete set of spare tools. Carpenters were needed to prepare much of the equipment placed in a tomb, above all the coffin which in Meketre's time was usually a masterpiece of the joiner's art.

To wait on Meketre in his posthumous existence servants would be needed. So three models representing attendants were included in the collection. Two are tall serving girls, each carrying a duck in one hand and balancing a basket on her head. One basket contains jars of beer, and the other holds various joints of meat and other food offerings. The third model consists of a group of four servants, two men and two women. The first man carries a jar of water for ritual libations and a censer for burning incense; the second supports a pile of linen sheets on his head. Each woman carries a goose in one hand, and with the other holds a basket on her head; the basket of the first woman contains wine jars and conical loaves of bread, while that of the second woman is filled with square loaves. Meketre did not have to worry about having to raise a finger in the after-life. He would be well looked after.

The remaining twelve models were all of boats of different kinds, some intended for the use of Meketre himself, and others designed for special functions connected with the way of life he would follow after death. Ancient Egyptians saw the land of the after-life completely in terms of the land of Egypt. So a River Nile ran through the domain of the dead and, like the Nile of the living, it was a highway, a place of recreation and a source of food. Four boats were for travelling. They all have cabins for their distinguished owner, and in one case the sail is raised, indicating that the boat is sailing upstream propelled by the prevailing wind from the north. Meketre sits with his son enjoying the journey, entertained by a small band of musicians. When he travelled in state Meketre was accompanied by a flotilla of attendant boats, two of which, both kitchen boats, were included in the collection. Everyone on board these boats is busy preparing the next meal, making bread, brewing beer, butchering meat, so that there need be the least delay between arriving at the destination and the serving of the food. One kitchen boat is being rowed and the other originally had a raised sail; one for travelling downstream and one for sailing upstream.

Four boats of smaller and lighter design, fitted with awnings, were replicas probably of the boats used for short journeys and for sedate pleasure cruises. An even lighter boat was to be used for hunting and fishing. It contains men ready to harpoon fish, nets for bird-catching and for fishing. Meketre and his son sit amidships watching the activities of the hunters as the boat is propelled along

The fishing rafts with a net slung between them.

by six men with paddles. The food provided by expeditions in this boat could be supplemented by the fish caught by the crews of two light papyrus rafts with a fishing net slung between them. Meketre would indeed be able to make full use of the river in the after-life with twelve boats at his disposal.

This wonderful collection of models from Meketre's supposedly empty tomb are not great works of art; they are not covered with or accompanied by informative inscriptions; yet they tell us more about daily life in ancient Egypt and of the methods of certain craftsmen than many much grander discoveries. Winlock was to continue working at Thebes for another ten years, and he was to find a great many important things, and some great works of Egyptian art. But nothing he found stirs the imagination and peoples it with lively scenes of ordinary, simple ancient Egyptians going about the activities of their everyday life like this set of models. How fortunate that his conscience nagged him into clearing out an already excavated tomb, just to draw the plan!

6

The Expulsion
of the Hyksos

What is known of the history of ancient Egypt depends almost
entirely on what has been found in the modern exploration of
Egypt, both by excavation and by the examination of inscriptions
on monuments above ground. Some periods have become relatively
well known because much material has been found to provide good
evidence of what went on. Other periods are very poorly known,
particularly the two so-called Intermediate Periods. One of the
chief reasons why so little is known of these periods is the absence
of major monuments dating from those times. They were periods
of weakness, when central authority could not be exerted efficiently.
At such times the country of Egypt easily split up into small,
almost independent units. Then the ruling house could display
only a shadowy authority, and could never undertake great works.
In fact they were periods without distinction, and as such they are
memorialised by few records of any consequence.

Nevertheless, even in these periods, people lived, worked,
fought and died, and an historian who wants to have a complete
picture of the country he studies, will make use of the most humble
evidence to help him understand what went on. When the narrative
of events is unclear, the historian has great opportunities to make
judgements and to use his powers of interpretation. He may seize
on some trifling fact or miserable object, and so squeeze it for sense
that the result is pure distortion. There are many cases in the
history of Egyptology where scholars have drawn dramatic conclusions from inadequate evidence, only to be proved wrong by
subsequent discoveries. The judicious handling of evidence is the
mark of a reliable scholar; the brilliant deduction, later confirmed,
is the mark of genius.

Aerial view of the temple of Amon-Re at Karnak.

So far the subjects discussed have all involved discoveries in the field of excavation. The lottery of the spade is strange and unpredictable. A promising site may yield nothing, a casual clearance may reveal wonders. But the gamble in excavation rarely lies in the intention of the excavator. He will dig for knowledge, and hope to find objects. What lies beneath the surface cannot be predicted. Yet a notable discovery, an unrobbed tomb, or a fine piece of sculpture, will bring the excavator a reputation often undeserved by standards based on intention rather than achievement. More often the value of what an excavator finds will only emerge after long study and the work of perhaps many scholars assessing and reassessing the evidence. Discovery in the study or in the museum is usually undramatic and the result of long thought; but what is discovered in this way may sometimes completely change what is thought of a subject. Let us here examine one topic where isolated discoveries have over the years helped to build up the picture.

During the Second Intermediate Period, between the Middle Kingdom and the New Kingdom, Egypt fell very largely under the rule of the Hyksos. Manetho describes how in the end the princes of Thebes revolted, drove back the Hyksos to Avaris, their stronghold and capital city in the Delta. Here they were besieged for many years until in the end the Egyptian king concluded a treaty with them and the Hyksos departed unmolested into Asia. Until fairly recent times Manetho's account was accepted, with reservations by good historians, as a reasonable statement of what might have happened. There was nothing to be found in Egyptian records of the actual period to confirm or to disprove Manetho's story. The only document known was not thought to provide any more trustworthy evidence. This was part of a romance preserved on a roll of papyrus, a paper-like material prepared by the Egyptians from the pith of the stem of the papyrus plant.

This papyrus, written during the Nineteenth Dynasty, perhaps four hundred years after the events it apparently described, is now in the British Museum. The first portion contains the beginning of a composition now known as *The Story of Apophis and Seqenenre*. In it the author describes the divided state of Egypt during the time of the Hyksos, and he reports how the Hyksos king Apophis picked a quarrel with the Theban king Seqenenre. He sent a message from Avaris to Thebes requiring Seqenenre to stop molesting the hippopotami in the palace pools there, because the noise of their roaring kept him awake at night. This ridiculous complaint could only be taken as a trumped up excuse for starting a war, although some subtle religious reasons may have been behind it. If Seqenenre went hunting the hippopotami with harpoons he could be enacting the old legend in which the god Horus (the living king) harpooned the evil god Seth in his guise as a hippopotamus. Furthermore, the special god of the Hyksos was that very Seth. So there may have been more behind Apophis' complaint than appears at first sight. Unfortunately the story breaks off just at the point when hostilities are about to start. Scholars have suggested that if the whole story had been preserved it would have told how Seqenenre ultimately triumphed over the Hyksos.

Eager to seize on any scrap of evidence that might confirm such a general account of events, Egyptologists were delighted by the discovery in 1881 of the mummy of Seqenenre. In that year a collection of royal mummies was found in a tomb near Deir el-Bahri to which they had been moved in antiquity to save them from complete destruction at the hands of robbers. The mummies were robbed of their fine funerary trappings, but were mostly otherwise in a fairly reasonable state of preservation. The mummy of Seqenenre, however, was very much an exception. The body itself was twisted and distorted, and there were the marks of serious wounds on his neck and skull. He had died undoubtedly as the result of violent action. Scholars were not slow to connect the nature of Seqenenre's death with the possibility that he had waged war against the Hyksos king Apophis. In no time it was being suggested that Seqenenre had fallen on the field of battle, and that his pitiful remains were gathered up and reverently prepared for burial by his sorrowing followers.

It was subsequently noticed that the most damaging wounds on Seqenenre's head occurred on the back of the skull. Clearly he had been attacked from behind. Was his camp taken by surprise? Was the king killed before he could even turn to defend himself? These suggestions on the whole seemed unlikely, so it was proposed that blows from behind indicated an attack by stealth. Therefore, was Seqenenre the victim of a conspiracy? In this way are myths developed, and photographs of the mummy of Seqenenre are often baldly stated to show the corpse of the king who had died in battle, or had been struck down by traitors.

Some doubt, however, must be cast even on Seqenenre's role in the liberation movement of the Seventeenth Dynasty. The length of his reign is not known; from his mummy his age at death may be estimated as about thirty. He was succeeded by his son Kamose, of whose part in the war against the Hyksos there can be no doubt. This fact was first revealed in a small discovery of quite unusual interest made in 1908 by the Earl of Carnarvon and Howard Carter. Since 1907 they had been working in the Theban necropolis just to the east of Deir el-Bahri. One of the tombs discovered by them in 1908 produced very little in the way of objects. It could be dated by its contents, mostly pottery, to the Seventeenth Dynasty. On a ledge they found a writing board and fragments of a second board.

The Egyptian writing board consisted of a piece of flat, thin wood, rounded at the corners and edges, covered with a layer of fine plaster which was smoothly finished. Such boards could be used for occasional writing, for taking notes, making copies, practising writing; they may have been used by student scribes. One end was pierced with a small hole through which string could be passed, and it is certain that they could in this way be hung up when not in use. Old texts could be wiped off with a damp cloth and the board reused for new texts. They performed much the same function as the old-fashioned school slate, or the modern

Head of the mummy of Seqenenre, showing some of the wounds which caused his death.

kitchen slate used to jot down kitchen memoranda. Examples of writing boards found in the past carried parts of literary texts, so it was no surprise to find that the complete board found at Thebes by Carter and Carnarvon had on one side of it the beginning of a semi-philosophical text dating from much earlier times. On the other side was the start of another composition which was not known before. Both texts were written in black ink in the script called hieratic which had a relationship to hieroglyphics something like that of modern handwriting to printing.

Although the text on the board, now known as Carnarvon Tablet No. 1, was published in 1912, the first proper study of it was made in 1916 by a young English scholar, Alan H. Gardiner. He had already made his mark in Egyptology as a master of Egyptian grammar, and as a brilliant decipherer of documents in the hieratic script. The text on Carnarvon Tablet No. 1 provided a fine challenge as a job of decipherment, and a teasing problem of interpretation. It starts with a date—Year 3 of King Kamose (about 1575 BC)—and a description given by Kamose to his council

68

of the state of Egypt at this time. In the north are the Hyksos; their capital is Avaris and their rule extends south to the town of Cusæ in Middle Egypt. At Thebes Kamose rules, and his control extends from Cusæ south to Elephantine at the First Cataract of the Nile. To the further south lies the domain of the prince of Kush. Kamose declares his eagerness to liberate Egypt from the Hyksos yoke, but his nobles counsel peace. They do not find the situation intolerable; they are even able to send their cattle north to the Delta for pasturing—a state of affairs which suggests fairly settled political conditions. However, Kamose's will prevails and he attacks northwards, his own Egyptian forces being reinforced by Nubian mercenaries. His first onslaughts on the town of Nefrusy are successful; what happens thereafter is unknown, for the text breaks off at this point.

What was this text? Could it be part of another romance like *The Story of Apophis and Seqenenre*? When was it written? What reliance could be put on it as an historical document? There was no doubt in Gardiner's mind that he was dealing with something much more authentic than a fictional account. Kamose was the last king of the Seventeenth Dynasty. The tomb from which the writing board came was of the Seventeenth Dynasty. The hieratic writing on the board was of the kind used in the late Seventeenth Dynasty. So there could be little doubt that the text should be dated also to the Seventeenth Dynasty. It could therefore have been written only during the reign of Kamose, or possibly shortly afterwards. Gardiner could also speak with authority on the language of the text, and of the way in which it was composed. He felt sure that it was the beginning of an official royal account of the start of the campaign against the Hyksos which was composed in Kamose's lifetime. Such an account would undoubtedly have been carved on a large commemorative slab, known to Egyptologists as a stela, and set up in the principal Theban temple. At some moment, probably soon after the raising of this slab, an Egyptian scribe or student-scribe chose to copy the opening lines of the text as an exercise, turning the hieroglyphs of the original into hieratic. He did not do a very good job, for Gardiner remarks: 'It is the work of a very careless and ignorant copyist, and abounds in smudges, alterations and ambiguities of all sorts.'

Gardiner was, therefore, strongly of the opinion that the text should be treated as an historical document, and its contents regarded as a truthful account of actual events, but only to the

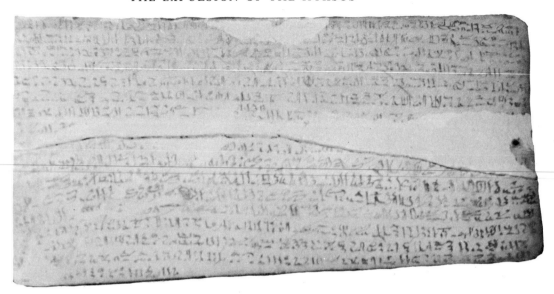

The Carnarvon
Tablet with the
beginning of the text
describing the initial
stages of the campaign
by Kamose to expel
the Hyksos from
Egypt.

extent to which Egyptian royal inscriptions could normally be
treated as truthful. Egyptian kings were inclined to be boastful in
their public statements, and in the memorial stelae they set up to
record their triumphs. So the historian should always be cautious
when using such texts as evidence. In the case of Kamose's text,
however, the very circumstantial and detailed character of the
narrative seemed to Gardiner to invest it with greater reliability
than usual. For him it became a document of prime historical
importance, and this opinion he maintained strongly in opposition
to the view that the text was a romantic story. The vindication of
Gardiner's point of view came in 1935 when French archaeologists
discovered in the great temple of Amon-Re at Karnak fragments of
a limestone stela inscribed with parts of a text which turned out to
be identical with that on Carnarvon Tablet No. 1. Unfortunately
not enough of the slab was recovered to add much of significance
to what was already preserved on the writing board. But one thing
was certain at last: the text on the board was a copy of an original
royal inscription, and consequently should be treated as an historical
document. Confirmation of a theory based on sound, though
slightly tenuous evidence, rarely comes so conclusively.

So a few more facts were confidently added to the history of the
last years of the Second Intermediate Period. Gradually the picture
of the expulsion of the Hyksos was being sketched in. It often
happens in archaeology, and indeed very frequently in Egyptology,

that an unexpected discovery contributes more to solving a problem than years of patient, scholarly work. In the story of the downfall of the Hyksos, the biggest discovery came as recently as 1954.

Again the scene is set in the temple of Amon-Re at Karnak. This temple, the site of an important shrine for many hundreds of years, saw great changes in the course of its history. The necessity to build, to increase or add to what already existed, constantly obliged successive Egyptian kings to destroy what their predecessors had built. 'Destroy' is not quite the right word, for what was dismantled of an old building was commonly reused in the new building. Sometimes a great formal doorway, known as a pylon, needed packing ballast to fill the space between the outer walls; whole buildings might be pulled down to provide the blocks for packing. Sometimes a court needed to be levelled or paved; what could be better for this purpose than the great slabs used for inscriptions by earlier kings? The fragments of Kamose's inscription or stela, found in 1935, came out of one of the great pylons in the Karnak temple. From the vast first court of Karnak came a second stela of Kamose in 1954.

Work of consolidation and repair is always in hand at Karnak. In 1954 the Chief Inspector of Antiquities in Upper Egypt, Dr Labib Habachi, had undertaken the examination of the foundations of a great statue in the first court. His architect, Dr M. Hammad, discovered that there were many reused blocks of earlier kings beneath the statue, so it was decided to examine the foundations of another statue nearby. It was under this statue that they found the second Kamose stela, a piece of limestone seven feet six inches high and three feet seven inches wide. Providentially it had escaped serious damage, and the thirty-eight lines of hieroglyphic text were almost entirely intact.

Egyptian royal inscriptions usually start in a very formal manner, often with a date and with a long declaration of the names and titles of the king concerned. Quite unusually the text on this new stela launches immediately into narrative, as if it continues a story begun on another stela. It has been sensibly suggested that Kamose had the account of his campaign against the Hyksos written up to cover two stelae, the first of which is now represented only by the fragments from the pylon and the copy on Carnarvon Tablet No. 1. The two stelae may have originally been set up on either side of a doorway leading into the temple of Amon-Re.

Much must have happened after the capture of Nefrusy in

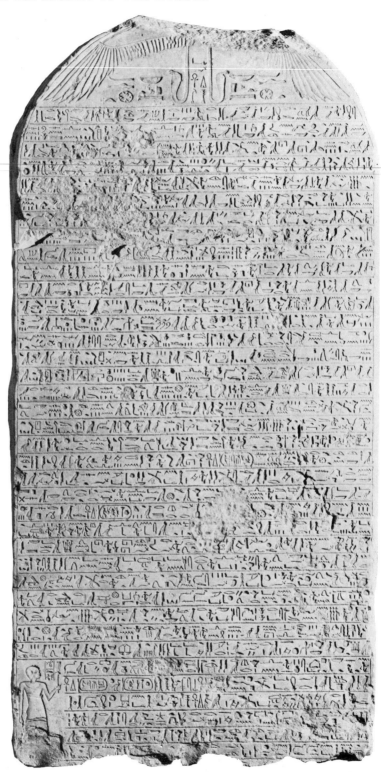

The Kamose Stela.
The inscription contains a continuation
of the account of
Kamose's campaign
against the Hyksos.

Kamose's first assault. The story of events given on the second stela does not follow an obvious sequence. Near the beginning some details are given of a raid deep into Hyksos territory in which warfare was carried right up to the walls of Avaris, the Hyksos capital. Kamose describes the devastation of the neighbourhood of Avaris by his forces and the insults that were hurled at his beleaguered enemies. Avaris did not fall on this occasion, and the next action described takes place in Middle Egypt. Kamose's men captured the messenger sent by Apophis to his ally, the prince of Kush; thus were the enemy's plans made clear to Kamose. The text of the actual letter sent by Apophis to the prince of Kush is quoted on the stela. To prevent a link-up between the forces of Avaris and Kush, Kamose sent a detachment into the Western Desert to seize an oasis lying on the route by which the Kushite force would march north. At this point the campaign season came to an end because of the inundation of the Nile, and Kamose withdrew his forces further south. The text on the stela ends with an account of the joy with which the news of the victory over the Hyksos was received in Thebes.

The second Kamose stela is quite remarkable. Not only does it recount events otherwise unknown, but it does so with a wealth of detail and an informality of language wholly unexpected in a royal inscription. It is a boastful text, but it is not disagreeably boastful, as so many later royal texts are; for its story is heroic, not bombastic. The struggle described is that of a king hoping to liberate his country; so many later texts are devoted to imperial conquests and the heroism purveyed in them is false and empty.

It is not impossible that further discoveries will reveal more of the struggle against the Hyksos. It is possible that Kamose died before another season of campaign arrived. His successor was Amosis, his younger brother, who finally drove the Hyksos out of Egypt, and is regarded as the first king of the Eighteenth Dynasty. A few details of the last campaigns are contained in the inscriptions preserved in tombs of military officials at El-Kab, south of Thebes. But the full accounts of the ultimate triumph remain to be discovered. If they ever turn up, it will be the task of the scholars in their studies, the successors of Alan Gardiner (who was later made Sir Alan Gardiner for his great contributions to scholarship) to find out precisely what they mean, to what extent they may be trusted, and what conclusions may be drawn from them.

7

A Golden Burial

In June 1914 the Earl of Carnarvon was granted the concession to excavate in the Valley of the Kings at Thebes. Up to that time the concession had been held by Theodore Davis, a rich American, who had come to the conclusion that there was no longer anything of importance to be found in the Valley. Why then were the Earl of Carnarvon and his associate Howard Carter so eager to obtain the right to dig in what might turn out to be a barren area? Something of the history of the Valley of the Kings needs to be told to provide the background for their intentions.

Early in the Eighteenth Dynasty the officials responsible for royal burials sought out a remote rocky valley in the Western Desert to act as the royal necropolis. The knowledge that tombs, whether royal or non-royal, were liable to be robbed, often not long after burials were made, obliged tomb officials to seek constantly for better ways of ensuring their continued safety from robbers. It would be hoped that in the new valley things would be better. It was a close place, difficult to enter and easy to guard. Here, if the necropolis police did their job properly, there might be some chance that the great kings would continue to lie in peace.

It has never been established for whom the first tomb was prepared. It ought to have been for Amenophis I, the second king of the Eighteenth Dynasty, because in later times he was specially revered by the workmen who cut the royal tombs in the Valley. But the earliest tomb so far discovered was made for Amenophis I's successor, Tuthmosis I. In the spring of 1914 Carnarvon and Carter had found a tomb in the Theban necropolis, but some distance from the Valley of the Kings, which they attributed to

74

Amenophis I. The evidence of ownership was slight, and few scholars now think that it was truly the tomb of that king. Nevertheless, its discovery, coming as it did at that time, excited the excavators and made them even more anxious to obtain the concession to work in the Valley where, Carter was convinced, there were surely undiscovered royal tombs to be found.

The royal tombs in the Valley are all externally insignificant compared with the pyramids and the other tombs of kings from earlier periods. They consist of corridors cut straight into the rock face, opening out into chambers, and descending by stairways to further corridors and chambers. Given strong doors and good police protection, they should have been easy to protect. But unfortunately the planners who chose the Valley did not make sufficient allowance for the ingenuity and determination of the tomb robbers, or for the likelihood that the necropolis police might be bribed. By Roman times many of the tombs already lay open to visitors, and from the scribbles written on the walls they had clearly become items on the guided tours of the period.

View of the Valley of the Kings while work was in progress on the tomb of Tutankhamun. In the foreground is the entrance to the tomb of Ramesses VI, and below are the steps to the entrance to Tutankhamun's tomb.

As a royal burial-place the Valley continued in use to the end of the Twentieth Dynasty (about 1085 BC). By this time the Egyptian ruling house was about to abandon Thebes as its capital, and the kings of the Twenty-first Dynasty ruled from and were buried in the Delta. During this dynasty a terrible scandal broke in Thebes. A commission was set up to examine the royal tombs, and it was found that many had been robbed. Some of the documents dealing with the commission and the legal proceedings which subsequently were instituted have been preserved. The evidence given by some of the robbers shows that the thefts in royal and other tombs were

carried out by quite humble workmen. There was no evidence of big syndicates of thieves operating on a large scale. As a result of the discoveries made in the course of the investigations the bodies of the kings which had survived were gathered together, rewrapped, and buried again in a tomb originally made for a Queen Inhapi, wife of Amosis the founder of the Eighteenth Dynasty. It was this collection of royal reburials which was found in 1881, and contained the pitiful remains of King Seqenenre. The bodies of many of the most famous kings of the Eighteenth, Nineteenth and Twentieth Dynasties were included in the collection. There could be no doubt that their tombs, even if they had not yet been discovered, had been pillaged in antiquity.

In spite of so much evidence pointing to the comprehensive activities of the ancient tomb robbers, excavators have always been drawn to the Valley of the Kings. Even if a particular king's tomb may have been robbed, the tomb itself would be worth discovering for the carved and painted reliefs and inscriptions it contained. Furthermore, ancient robbers often left quite a lot behind them, especially if they were interrupted in their work. At the beginning of this century excavators had in mind the example of the Italian Giovanni Belzoni who had discovered the tomb of Sethos I of the Nineteenth Dynasty in 1817. The tomb was robbed, but its wall decorations were splendid and, for the most part, splendidly preserved.

More recently greater encouragement had been provided by the excavations of Theodore Davis, for whom Howard Carter himself had worked for a time. Davis found the robbed tombs of several kings and non-royal personages, and in particular, in a side valley off the main Valley, the unrobbed tomb of Yuia and Tjuiu, father and mother of Tiy, the wife of Amenophis III. The fine tomb furniture discovered here was the nearest thing to a royal equipment of the New Kingdom so far recovered, and it gave a wonderful idea of what might be found if an undisturbed king's tomb were ever unearthed. The dream of such a find was undoubtedly the principal reason why Carnarvon and Carter so eagerly desired the concession to dig in the Valley.

From years of working in the Theban necropolis, Carter had developed a fine instinct for potentially rewarding sites. With the opportunity to work again in the Valley of the Kings he did not hesitate to pitch his expectations on a high level. He did not under-estimate the difficulties, chiefly caused by the great dumps of rock

View into the
Antechamber, showing
the confusion of
tomb equipment.
On the left the king's
chariots, *on the right*
pieces of furniture
and boxes containing
food offerings.

chippings from the work of earlier excavators, but he was never
prepared to concede that there remained nothing to find. In
particular, and he maintained this view strongly in later years, he
hoped to find the tomb of Tutankhamun, a king of the late Eighteenth
Dynasty, about whom very little was known. This king's body had
not been found along with the other royal mummies in Inhapi's
tomb, but there were several pieces of evidence which suggested
that he had been buried in the Valley. All this evidence came from
discoveries made by Theodore Davis. In one place he had found a
faience cup inscribed with the name of Tutankhamun; in another
he had uncovered a small pit containing, among other things,
fragments of gold foil bearing the names of Tutankhamun and of
his queen, Ankhesenamun. Davis maintained that the pit was
actually Tutankhamun's tomb, but this claim could not be treated
seriously. The most significant discovery, however, was another
small pit filled with large pottery jars. These contained what
appeared to be rubbish—fragments of pottery, pieces of linen,
remains of floral collars, and other odds and ends. Davis considered

77

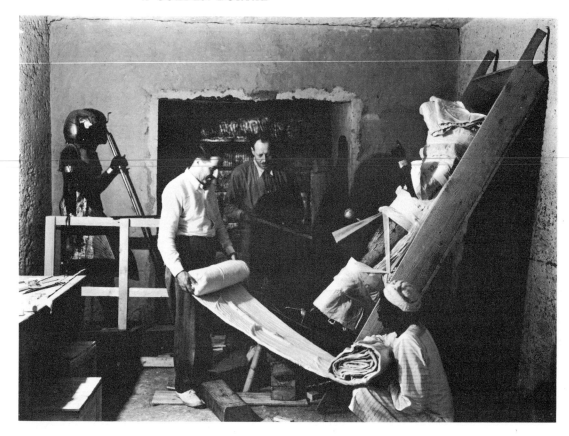

Carter and his assistants prepare to move one of the two guardian statues of the king from the entrance to the Burial Chamber. In the background the gilded outermost shrine can be seen.

them of no interest and allowed Herbert Winlock, who later became the excavator of the tomb of Meketre, to carry them off to New York. On studying the contents of the jars Winlock came to the conclusion that they made up the refuse left over after the completion of the burial ceremonies of Tutankhamun. His name occurred on several items, and in the ink inscriptions on the jars. Winlock's conclusions meant that Tutankhamun had undoubtedly been buried in the Valley, and that the tomb should not be far from the spot where the funerary material had been buried.

From the clues provided by these earlier discoveries Carter concluded that the king's tomb should lie somewhere in the centre of the Valley of the Kings. Plans were drawn up for a large-scale operation in the season 1914–15, but the outbreak of the First World War led to their cancellation. It was not until 1917 that Carter was able to begin work seriously. With Lord Carnarvon he planned a strategy. They should concentrate their work in a triangle, the angles of which were marked by the tombs of the kings Ramesses II, Merenptah and Ramesses VI. Before a serious investigation of the unexamined floor of the Valley in this triangle could be undertaken, formidable masses of debris had to be shifted. In the first season good progress in general clearance was made, and one interesting find consisted of a group of ancient workmen's huts just below the entrance to the tomb of Ramesses VI. The presence of such huts anywhere in the Valley usually indicated the proximity of a royal tomb, but their closeness to the tomb of Ramesses VI deterred Carter from moving them and investigating further. In so doing he would have made access to the tomb of Ramesses VI impossible, and that would have been very unpopular with tourists. So, for the time being, the huts were left in position.

For the next four seasons the slow clearance continued. Small finds brought slight relief to the ever-hopeful excavators, but the long-awaited great find remained elusive. In the summer of 1922, after an especially depressing season's work, the Earl of Carnarvon felt that the time had come to call a halt. He discussed the matter with Carter who had little to offer as positive encouragement to continue the work. Still, Carter did not want to give up without a final try, even if he himself had to pay the workmen. Carnarvon, however, agreed to finance one more season, but that would be all. Carter was delighted; his plan was to start early, and to dig beneath the group of workmen's huts. By so doing he hoped to give as little trouble as possible to visitors to the tomb of Ramesses VI. He might have finished before the tourist season got well under way.

As soon as he had reached Luxor he put his workmen to begin on the area of the huts. After two days' work a good record had been made of the remains of these simple structures, and they were removed in preparation for an examination of the ground below them. The huts themselves had been built on a layer of debris which overlaid the actual valley floor. It was unlikely that there would in fact be anything in the floor itself, but no part of the concession was to be left unexplored. When Carter arrived on the dig on the morning of November 4 he sensed immediately that something was afoot from the unusual silence—so different from the workmen's characteristic chatter. Apparently, the first trench dug had immediately hit a step cut in the rock floor.

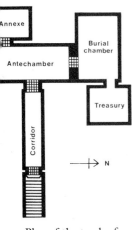

Plan of the tomb of Tutankhamun

Quickly the area round about was cleared, and a cutting in the rock was revealed, into which led a flight of steps. It took a day to clear away enough of the debris to allow them with safety to carry their investigations deeper. Carter was already sure that he had found the entrance to a tomb, but he was puzzled about its nature because of its unusual position so low down in the floor of the Valley. By the evening of November 5 the workmen had cleared down to the twelfth step, and there they reached the top of what was undoubtedly the plastered-up entrance to the tomb. On the small area of doorway uncovered Carter could see the seals of the royal necropolis authorities; but no impressions containing a royal name could be found. Making a small hole at the level of the lintel, he was able to see that the space behind was filled completely with rubble. All the indications therefore were that the tomb was intact. One thing that was certain was that it must have contained the burial of an important person to warrant the use of the royal necropolis seal. It also followed, from the presence of the workmen's huts above, which could be dated to the Twentieth Dynasty, that nothing below the huts could have been disturbed since they were built in about 1150 BC. Hopes ran high in Carter's camp on the evening of November 5. But ever mindful of Lord Carnarvon's personal interest, Carter refilled the stairway cutting and telegraphed to England, 'At last have made wonderful discovery in Valley; a magnificent tomb with seals intact; re-covered same for your arrival, congratulations.'

With what was unusual speed for those days, Carnarvon arrived in Egypt on November 20, and on the 23rd he reached Luxor. Work was resumed at once, and on the 24th the whole stair was uncovered. Sixteen steps led down to the sealed door. Now that it could be seen in its entirety, other seals bearing the name of Tutankhamun could be observed. What also could be seen—and this was very disquieting—was that the doorway had been broken through in more than one place and had later been resealed. Plunderers therefore had entered the tomb. How much damage had they done? Presumably not too much, otherwise the necropolis authorities would not have bothered to reseal the entrance.

On the following day, after the doorway with its sealings had been photographed and carefully recorded, it was broken down, and the passage beyond tackled. As the rubble packing was removed, many fragments of small objects were discovered, which were presumably things dropped by the robbers. Gradually the passage descended into the rock, and its end was not reached until the afternoon of the next day, November 26, the day which was to be for Carter the most wonderful he had ever lived through. After thirty feet, the passage ended in another plastered doorway. Like the first, it bore seal impressions of Tutankhamun and of the royal

OPPOSITE
The mummy of Tutankhamun exposed in its coffin. Each piece of jewellery was numbered by Carter for record purposes.

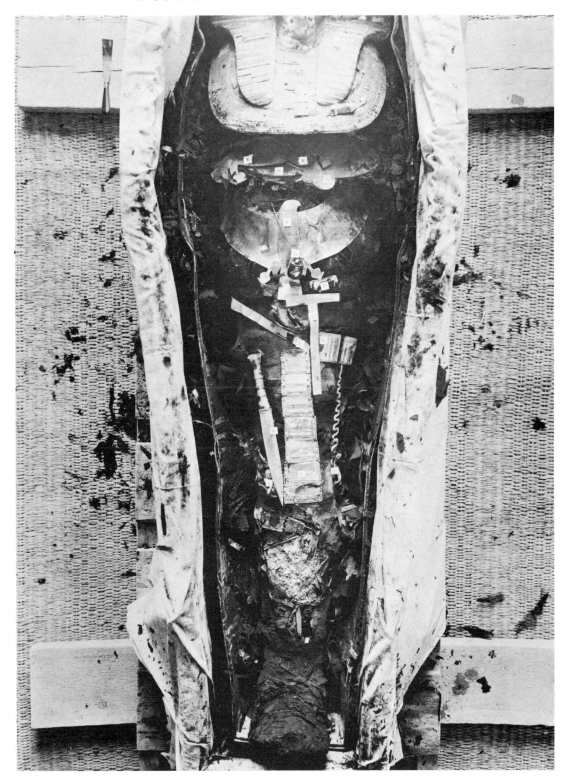

necropolis authorities; like the first, there were obvious signs of earlier entry, and of resealing. The depressing trail of fragments and the sure signs of robbery on the doorways had by now convinced the excavators that their find might not be all they had once thought it might be. Indeed, would it be a tomb or just a cache of funerary equipment rescued from various plundered tombs? No one could foretell what lay behind the second door; but in spite of their fears the excavators remained full of expectation. The first breach in the doorway was made by Carter, in the top, left-hand corner. The hot air within the chamber beyond almost put out his candle as he inserted it, but as the flame became steady he saw an amazing sight—a room full of objects, strange animals, tumbled furniture, and everywhere, the glint of gold. At last Carnarvon impatiently said, 'Can you see anything?' With difficulty Carter replied, 'Yes, wonderful things.'

In the account of the discovery written by Carter shortly after the end of the 1922–23 season, and long before the full scale of what was to come from the tomb was known, he constantly emphasises the feelings of wonder and awe which gripped all those concerned with the discovery. The excavation took on a new dimension. The excavators were now fully aware that they had made a discovery of unique importance. The thrill was immense, but so too was the realisation of the responsibility which lay on the shoulders of all who were to work on the tomb. They had to deal with material of a kind never before found, and all they did would take place under a blaze of publicity. Stresses not normally experienced by excavators would be experienced. There was indeed much food for thought in the situation.

A great deal has been said in earlier chapters of the caution with which good excavators approach their work. So many considerations have to be taken into account when a big task of clearance is undertaken. Most of the problems were magnified many times over in the case of Tutankhamun's tomb. Happily Howard Carter was in every way suited to handle the situation. He was not only an excavator of flair and imagination, but a man of great practical aptitudes, capable of dealing efficiently with the many difficult problems of recovery and conservation which needed to be solved in the course of clearing the tomb. He had a masterly eye for detail, a skilled understanding of technical matters, an assurance based on years of experience working in royal and private tombs at Thebes, and an artist's ability to draw on paper precisely what was

The unwrapped feet of the mummy of the king, wearing gilded sandals. Each toe is encased by a small gold sheath.

significant of the strange and wonderful things which emerged from the tomb.

After the first opening of the tomb and the astonished viewing of the jumbled contents of the first chamber, which was called the Antechamber, a period of sober assessment and steady preparation followed. The mass of material in this room, although apparently in a good state, would need careful handling and individual treatment. The room could not be cleared like a house on removal day. And it was obvious that no further exploration of the tomb could take place until the Antechamber had been cleared. The magnitude of Carter's discovery inevitably drew many offers of help from others, but of all the possibilities, the most practical came from the Metropolitan Museum expedition working over the hill at Deir el-Bahri. And of the Metropolitan staff, the one who became the most vital and useful for Carter was Harry Burton, the photographer who had been the first at the discovery of Meketre's cache of models. His skill and experience provided Carter in due time with a wonderful photographic record of his find.

Another invaluable piece of assistance took the form of the loan

83

Gilded wooden figure
of Tutankhamun
wearing the crown of
Lower Egypt

by the Egyptian Antiquities Service of the tomb of Sethos II in
the Valley as a store and workshop to which the objects could be
taken as they were removed from the tomb. Here, in conditions of
peace and security—for the tomb of Sethos II was tucked away in a
relatively unvisited corner of the Valley—essential first-aid work
could be carried out on damaged and unstable objects before they
were removed from Thebes to Cairo. The daily convoy of wooden
trays loaded with priceless objects from the new tomb to the old,
became a regular tourist attraction in the Valley, for which the
crowds would gather to gape.

From the first it was obvious to the excavators that more rooms
lay beyond the Antechamber. Two life-sized wooden statues of the
king stood guard over another blocked door which, like the others,
showed signs of having been breached at some time. But the
clearance of the Antechamber had to precede any penetration
beyond; so with stoic restraint the tasks of noting, photographing
and removing the multifarious objects of the first room continued
until the whole room was empty, except for the two statues. One fact
that emerged clearly in the course of clearing the Antechamber was
that the plunderers had never succeeded in exploiting their entry.
While they had undoubtedly removed some objects from boxes,
and torn gold-covered elements from wooden furniture, the bulk
of the material had been left intact, and had been roughly tidied up
by the necropolis officials after the plunderers had been discovered.

The formal removal of the doorway between the two sentinel
statues took place on February 17 1923. A wall of gold was soon
revealed to the chosen group of spectators who had gathered in the
Antechamber—a sight never before seen by modern man, the
intact funerary shrine of a Pharaoh. In due course the extraordinary
elaboration of protection provided for the royal mummy was revealed. Four shrines of gilded wood, one inside each other, like
Chinese boxes, enclosed the great quartzite sarcophagus, which in
turn contained three coffins, two of gilded wood and one of solid
gold. Within the last and grandest coffin lay the mummy of the
king, decked out with all the trappings of royalty. On his head was
a wonderful gold mask, modelled in the features of the living king;
within the bandages and on the body itself were dozens of pieces of
jewellery, magical emblems and talismans, the necessary accoutre-
ment of sovereignty in death. And all this for a mere youth in his
late teens, whose rule, as far as we can tell, was undistinguished
and short. What would the burial of one of Egypt's greatest kings,

The gilded wooden shrine from the Treasury which contained the mummified internal organs of the king. Isis and Selkis, two of the protective goddesses, stand with outstretched arms to guard the contents.

like Ramesses II, have contained?

It is idle to speculate on what we shall never know. For Carter, Tutankhamun's tomb was more than enough. The Burial Chamber and a room beyond, the Treasury, containing many of the ritual objects closely connected with the royal mummy, and intimately involved in its posthumous existence, produced the most precious and unusual things in the tomb. The little Annexe, opening off the Antechamber, yielded a mass of incidental equipment, in itself marvellous, but of relative modesty compared with the contents of the two most important rooms.

The work of clearance and consolidation continued at Thebes until the spring of 1932. Progress had not wholly been harmonious and uninterrupted; clashes between Carter and the authorities of the Antiquities Service had at times made work in the tomb very

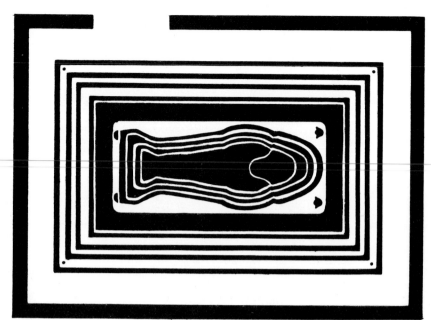

Plan of the Burial Chamber with the king's mummy enclosed within three coffins, a stone sarcophagus and four gilded wooden shrines

difficult and even led to one long stoppage. But the immediate task of emptying the tomb was by that year completed. The Earl of Carnarvon, himself the instigator, patron and inspiration of the excavation, had died in 1923 of a fever following a mosquito bite. The suddenness of his death gave substance to a story put about by an Egyptologist that a curse was attached to the tomb. A gullible public fastened eagerly on this story and over the years the idea of a malevolent influence has never ceased to be associated with the tomb and its contents. Yet most of the people concerned with the discovery lived on for many years. Carter himself survived until 1939, not altogether a satisfied man, in spite of the wonderful discovery he had made. He failed to write up his great collection of notes for publication; and since his death the years have sped by with little being directly achieved. The treasures from Tutankhamun's tomb remain unique, and an unimaginable source of information. The work of the excavators was carried out with the utmost care and devotion; the admirable condition of the objects, now to be seen in the Cairo Museum, is principally due to the systematic attention they received as they were brought from the tomb. But the labours of Carter will remain unfulfilled until the contents of the tomb have been properly studied and published, a duty which until recently has been shirked by Egyptologists. Now there is hope that the incomplete work will be completed. It will, if carried through, set the crown on Carter's achievement.

8

Makers of the
House of Eternity

The wonderful discoveries made in the tomb of Tutankhamun, unique and extraordinary as they are, have not taught us very much about life in ancient Egypt during the late Eighteenth Dynasty. Howard Carter and his fellow excavators had hoped that the tomb might contain papyrus rolls inscribed with all kinds of texts, but in fact nothing of the sort was discovered. The substantial inscriptions which covered the gilded shrines contained religious texts of kinds already known. You do not excavate a great temple to learn about the beliefs of simple people; so you should not expect to gain much insight into the daily life of simple people from the excavation of a royal tomb. But even as Carter was at work in the Valley of the Kings, discoveries were being made elsewhere at Thebes which transformed Egyptological studies in the very field of ancient everyday life.

If you had been a tourist visiting Thebes in the 1920s, your first desire would have been to glimpse inside Tutankhamun's tomb. What you might have chosen as your second target could have been selected from a long series of well-known monuments, from other royal tombs, the temple at Deir el-Bahri, the charming private tombs, or one of many similar antiquities. It is unlikely, however, that you would have taken the rocky track leading out of the Valley, over the hills, skirting the peak that dominates the Theban necropolis, and dropping down to another valley, now known as Deir el-Medina. Here, if you had bothered to make the journey, you would have found Bernard Bruyère, a French excavator, working away undramatically on a kind of back-yard site.

This part of the Theban necropolis, rather tucked away in the hills, lies about half-way between the Valley of the Kings and the district known as the Valley of the Queens where many queens and members of the royal families were buried during the New Kingdom. Deir el-Medina had been recognised for a hundred years as a place where interesting small antiquities might be found—nothing very dramatic, but the sorts of things which would form the bread-and-butter of a gentleman's private collection. Italian archaeologists had excavated there in the early years of this century and had discovered tombs and part of a village. Their concession had been taken over by the French Institute in Cairo. Right up until the Second World War, and for a few seasons after the war, Bruyère conducted annual campaigns in this valley, and laid bare the whole village and the tombs and other dependent buildings connected with it. The work was carried out meticulously; it received little publicity; but it produced so much material of a truly informative kind that still only part of its significance is understood.

This village at Deir el-Medina was the home of the workmen who had cut Tutankhamun's tomb, and all the others in the Valley of the Kings. If you had taken that rocky path from the Valley to the village you would have followed the very track by which the ancient workmen trailed back home on their rest days three thousand years ago. Still today, if you walk that path and keep your eyes open, you will see traces of that élite band among Egyptian workmen whose sole aim in life was to prepare a 'house of eternity' for their king. You will see some of their rough stone huts where they would

The workmen's village at Deir el-Medina.

spend the nights during their shifts of duty, for they only returned home to the village every ten days for a rest day; you may recognise tiny dry-stone shrines, now robbed of any sacred image or inscription, where they said their prayers, invoking foreign gods and local spirits, who were more accessible to simple folk than the great gods of the temples in Thebes. On some smooth surfaces among the rocks you can clearly see the scratched inscriptions, scribbled there by the passing workmen. These were no ordinary labourers, but skilled men, most of whom could read and write. You can sit and rest on a natural seat in a cleft of the rock and see where an ancient scribe has written up his name and reserved the spot as his own 'sitting-place'.

Down at Deir el-Medina was the little closed community which was the home of the workmen on the royal tombs. It formed a strange, select enclave in the vast necropolis area of Thebes; for us it has become a microcosm of Egyptian life. And by a miracle of preservation it survived in sufficiently good state until modern times to divulge many of its secrets to an excavator who took his time, slowly assembling the vast jig-saw puzzle of knowledge from thousands of fragments. What was discovered yields a story of life in almost monastic conditions.

The foundation of the village can be traced back at least to the reign of Tuthmosis I of the Eighteenth Dynasty (about 1520 BC), because bricks stamped with his name occur in the great wall which surrounds the village proper. You will remember from the last chapter that the earliest, certainly identified, royal tomb in the Valley of the Kings was made for Tuthmosis I. This fact, taken with the evidence of the stamped bricks, seems to suggest that this king was responsible for the setting up of the special squad of tomb workmen, and for basing them in their own secluded village. There is, however, good reason to suppose that the founding Pharaoh of the squad was Amenophis I, the immediate predecessor of Tuthmosis I; his tomb has never been discovered, although Carnarvon and Carter thought they had found it in 1914. The reason for thinking that Amenophis was the founder derives from the strong devotion shown to his memory, and to that of his mother, Ahmes Nefertari, by the workmen. Throughout the long history of the village, which continued to the end of the Twentieth Dynasty in active use, the successive generations of inhabitants numbered the cult of this king and his mother among the more reliable and accessible divine agencies to which they could direct their prayers.

Many small stelae have been found on which workmen are shown making adoration to the seated statues of Amenophis and Ahmes Nefertari. They were undoubtedly thought of as the patrons of the necropolis, probably because they had set up the organisation on which the workmen depended for their livelihood.

Unlike most inhabited parts of Egypt, the village at Deir el-Medina, being far from the cultivated areas, was not affected by the destructive influences of the annual inundation of the Nile, by sub-soil seepage of water, and by the regular rebuilding which affected most village and town sites. As a place for living Deir el-Medina was not ideal. It had no water, no land for cultivation, little shelter from the sun, and no pleasing prospect. Egyptians loved trees because they gave shade at midday; no trees could grow at Deir el-Medina. When it was founded the place was chosen probably because of its isolation, and even perhaps for some of its physical disadvantages. On the other hand, once established there, and provided by the king with all the needs of life, the conveniences of the situation would have become more apparent. It often happens that disagreeable conditions of life come to be so accepted that in

Tomb stela of Neferhotep, workman from Deir el-Medina. He is shown giving praise to the deceased king Amenophis I and his royal mother, Ahmes Nefertari.

time they become regarded as inseparable from the way of life 'enjoyed' by the sufferers; hence they become privileges. So with the occupants of the workmen's village, as time passed they jealously guarded their exclusive status and their possession of this uncomfortable village. The necropolis workmen were special, and they would not have changed their status willingly.

When the workmen's squad was first set up the idea of the village followed inevitably. It was to be both a home and almost a prison. The members of the squad, although skilled craftsmen, were only artisans, and had few natural privileges. But if they were to continue in royal service, it was necessary to keep them together as a gang. Settled together in a village with their families they would have less reason to defect and run away.

For the whole period of its existence the village remained within the original walls of brick built in the reign of Tuthmosis I. When Bernard Bruyère had completed his excavation, the plan of the village was clearly revealed; it extended about 145 yards in length and about fifty yards in width. Visitors to Deir el-Medina can still see the individual buildings and walk into the little houses once occupied by the painters, draughtsmen, sculptors, scribes and others, all of whom devoted their lives to the making of tombs for kings and members of the royal family. There are about seventy houses, built for the most part side by side and back to back. There is only one entrance into the village, on the north side, giving on to the one principal street which runs, not quite in a straight line, from north to south. There are a very few side paths, but in general the area within the walls is a solid mass of houses, not at all a planner's dream, but undoubtedly the framework of a real community. From the great quantities of small domestic and personal objects retrieved in the course of excavation it has been possible to identify the owners of many of the houses. Being able to write, the workmen put their names on all sorts of things which in other settlements would have remained uninscribed—pieces of household furniture, tools, domestic utensils even.

Apparently the houses tended to become family dwellings, handed on from generation to generation, just as workman sons would follow their workman fathers in the particular crafts in which they were expert. The houses are mostly of the same design; they are not very big, but would undoubtedly have been considered rather superior artisan dwellings in ancient Egypt. The foundations were of stone, their walls of mud brick, and their roofs of wood. In most you entered by a short stair into a reception room in which guests and visitors could be received. From there you moved into the living room which formed the focus of family life; here the family ate and passed the time in the long hours, even days, when the men might be away on duty in the Valley of the Kings. In this room too was a small niche in which a bust representing the protective family ancestral spirit was placed, the object of special family devotion. From this living room the smaller bedroom opened and by its side ran a short corridor to the kitchen where water, grain and other provisions were kept and where food was prepared. Usually each house was equipped with a cellar reached by a stair from the living room; another stair led from the rear of the house to a terrace on the roof—a place for sitting out when the day was not too hot, or for sleeping when the night was oppressive.

Such were the houses at Deir el-Medina. A few built outside the confines of the village are a little larger, but on the whole they all show a remarkable modesty which suggests that life in this community was lived without domestic competition. So it lasted for a period of four hundred years. In the hillside close by, the workmen made their tombs, and being well practised in the arts and crafts of tomb-making, they made their own houses of eternity almost as fine as those prepared elsewhere in the Theban necropolis for quite

The reconstructed superstructure in the form of a pyramid of the tomb of one of the workmen.

important officials. Like the houses, so the tombs in time became used by generation after generation as family sepulchres. The revelation of the communal character of this village with its burial ground was one of the most interesting results of Bruyère's excavations at Deir el-Medina. But the results were much magnified by the study of the vast numbers of written documents discovered in and about the village, and particularly in pits into which all kinds of waste material had been thrown in antiquity.

That the workmen were very literate has already been emphasised. The art of writing in the cursive hieratic script was certainly taught among the many skills required by the royal necropolis workmen. Students used writing boards like the Carnarvon Tablet No. 1, mentioned in Chapter 6, but more commonly they used flakes of limestone for writing exercises. Such flakes with writing on them are now called ostraca; they were used for all kinds of occasional writing, and frequently bear simple texts of a kind rarely found written out formally on papyrus. There are accounts, lists of food, inventories of materials, prayers to local gods, curses against enemies, questions to oracles, even caricatures of people. From such cast-away trifles much can be learned about people. Bruyère found many thousands of ostraca at Deir el-Medina, and their reading and interpretation were mostly carried out by Jaroslav Černý, a Czech Egyptologist who spent many years in Britain as a professor, first in London and later in Oxford.

Černý's knowledge of the language of the period and of the various styles of handwriting was so great that he could make out texts which were badly faded or even partly worn away. He knew the workmen by name, who their parents were, whom they married. From the intimate details on ostraca he often knew the background of their scandals, the reasons why occasionally they got into trouble with the senior necropolis officials. A very great deal of what we know now about the life of ordinary Egyptians comes from the researches of Bruyère and Černý on the discoveries at Deir el-Medina. It was indeed a special and favoured community, but it was not a community of important people whose lives were passed in pampered luxury, like the chancellor Meketre. They were hard-working craftsmen whose privileges in life were relatively modest.

In ancient times the village and its neighbourhood were called the Place of Truth, and the workmen were Servants in the Place of Truth on the West of Thebes. It is not at all clear why this name was given to the village, but it suggests that it was invested

Plan of a small shrine
drawn in black ink on
a pottery ostracon
from Thebes.

with some kind of religious character. It was something like a monastery in its exclusive nature, but it also had elements of a college in its communal methods of life. The workmen were paid in kind by regular distributions of rations which included grain for bread- and beer-making, fish, vegetables and oil. Water was brought regularly and allocated both in the village and in the places where the men worked; so too was wood for fuel; pottery was provided, for there were no local facilities for making pots. Certain services also were organised, like those of the laundry man whose duties were restricted to washing the linen of the workmen themselves; no doubt household linen was dealt with by the women of the individual households. While the provision of rations seems on the whole to have operated efficiently, and indeed the regular supplies were often supplemented on feast days, there were times when things went wrong, and the rations were not delivered. During the Twentieth Dynasty it is recorded that rations fell into arrears on several occasions; then the workmen went on strike and even marched in protest round the Theban necropolis to the offices of the administrative officials which were established at Medinet Habu in the enclosure of the mortuary temple of Ramesses III. Like any group of workmen whose services are special and valued, and, at least for the moment, irreplaceable, the Servants in the Place of Truth felt able to make a strong demonstration in support of their grievances.

While the workmen felt themselves to be privileged, they could not consider themselves to be above the ordinary law of the land in so far as their actions might transgress the established order. Between themselves their behaviour was regulated by a tribunal established within the village whenever a dispute occurred. The rules by which the tribunal was set up and according to which it conducted its business can only be guessed at. Probably it was a kind of council of representatives headed by an elder workman. In small matters this tribunal could settle cases and pass judgements, but in serious affairs the office of the vizir, the chief civil authority, would intervene. In fact the vizir was responsible ultimately for the work and welfare of the workmen's community.

All these details concerning the life of the workmen have emerged from the study of the written records found at Deir el-Medina. The same sorts of document give us also a very full picture of how the workmen went about their professional tasks. For most of its existence the gang of workmen amounted to about sixty persons. They were organised into two sections, each with its own foreman and deputy. The gang was called a 'crew' and the sections were termed the left and right 'sides' as if the two banks of rowers, one on each side of a boat, were being referred to. In their work the 'sides' operated according to their designations, one working down the left side of the tomb and the other down the right side. While the principal task of the whole 'crew' was to cut and decorate the tomb for the ruling king, they were also employed on the tombs for queens and important royal children.

They did all the work on the royal tomb from start to finish, once the place in which it was to be cut had been decided. The general lay-out of the tomb was probably determined at a high level, the king himself taking an interest in what was to be prepared for his mummy. A plan was prepared on papyrus and copies no doubt given to the foremen of the two 'sides' of the 'crew', to be used as their guides in the work. A plan on papyrus of the tomb of Ramesses IV with dimensions given can be seen in the Turin Museum, while a rough plan of the tomb of Ramesses IX on an ostracon is in the Cairo Museum. The ostracon plan came from the Valley of the

Kings and may have been discarded by one of the foremen after the tomb had been completed. A scribe worked with the foreman, supervising the work in the tomb. He was, in modern terms, the Clerk of Works. He made sure that work continued according to plan, noted how much was achieved each day, kept a record of absences, and in general was the vizir's watch-dog.

Limestone ostracon with an artist's sketch showing a king spearing a lion

The actual work on the tomb seems to have gone forward with remarkable speed when conditions were normal. Apart from the three rest days a month, and occasional festivals, the workmen were kept at their tomb without break. They lived on or near the job in spite of the fact that their village lay scarcely a mile away. Undoubtedly the severe discipline imposed was nothing unusual in the kind of society which existed in ancient Egypt at this time, and the workmen probably did not consider themselves particularly badly treated. The most arduous part of the whole task was the cutting of the corridors and chambers. Even so, a large royal tomb could be prepared to this extent in two years. The decoration of the tomb walls with the scenes and inscriptions required for traditional religious reasons took very much longer, and it often happened that a tomb was not finished when the king died. Burial had to be made according to a prescribed timetable, and there was no chance of finishing off the decoration subsequently. So if you ever visit the royal tombs in the Valley of the Kings, you will see in many places that only the preliminary drawings have been made on the tomb walls. In some places it indeed looks as if the painter or carver had just put down his implements for the midday break, and never come back in the afternoon.

If you ever do visit the Valley, spare a thought for the workmen who made the tombs, and don't forget to visit Deir el-Medina. Walk down the main street of the village, look into the house of Pashed who used to draw the designs on the walls of tombs; go into the cellar where Amennakhte kept his beer—he used to carve the inscriptions and representations on the tomb walls. Think of these humble, but talented, people, whose wonderful work is as much their memorial as it is of their royal masters. We know far more about the workmen than we do about the masters, and what we know is of such great interest. And all this knowledge is due to the careful work of Bernard Bruyère and Jaroslav Černý, the one in the field and the other in the study. Together they formed an ideal association of the practical and the theoretical; they truly have made the past live again.

9

The Problems of Tanis

A papyrus purchased in Cairo in 1891 and now in Moscow contains an account of a journey made in the last years of the Twentieth Dynasty by an official called Wenamun. He bore the resounding title 'elder of the portal of the estate of Amun, Lord of the Thrones of the Two Lands', and he set out from Thebes to travel to Syria to obtain cedar wood for the sacred boat of the god Amon-Re which was used on the Nile at Thebes to carry the sacred image of the god when it was taken in procession by land and water to visit other temples in the Theban area. The whole story of Wenamun's mission is full of incident, but for the moment it is of special interest to us because of the picture it gives of the state of affairs in Egypt round about 1100 BC.

Wenamun, it seems, had been sent on the orders of Hrihor, the High Priest of Amun, and his first important stopping place was the town of Tanis in the Delta, the place where, as Wenamun says, 'Smendes and Tentamun are'. He presented his credentials to Smendes and his wife, Tentamun, and they in due course equipped Wenamun for his voyage. Although the report of Wenamun does include a reference to the ruling Pharaoh of the time, the impression it gives is that Egypt was under the control of two separate authorities, Hrihor in the south, based on Thebes, and Smendes and Tentamun in the north, based on Tanis. This situation must have been developing for some time towards the end of the Twentieth Dynasty, and it must have produced some awkward moments. It is known that there was undoubtedly a Pharaoh in the land at this time, but at present nobody knows what kind of authority he wielded, or even where he lived.

Throughout the New Kingdom the centre of royal power in Egypt had moved more and more towards the north. This, perhaps, is not very surprising because so many of the interests of Egypt became bound up with events in Asia. A king residing in Thebes was many days further away from the Asiatic border of the land than a king based at Memphis or at a capital in the Delta. Ramesses II had founded a new royal residence in the Delta, and he called it the 'House of Ramesses' or 'Piramesse'. Scribes wrote accounts of its beauty and the advantages of its situation, and claimed that it was the only place worth living in in Egypt. There can be little doubt that many of the kings of the Nineteenth and Twentieth Dynasties spent most of their time at Piramesse, and only travelled to Thebes occasionally to attend some very important ceremony.

Inevitably, therefore, control at Thebes fell increasingly into the hands of the priesthood of Amun, the centre of whose power lay in the vast temple of Karnak. By the reign of Ramesses XI at the end of the Twentieth Dynasty, the High Priest of Amun, Hrihor, felt strong enough to act as if he were the temporal as well as the spiritual authority. Only in a few places within the confines of the great temple did he actually have his name written in a royal cartouche, but in other respects he ruled without any fear that his actions might be opposed or repudiated by Ramesses XI.

How the situation in the Delta had so deteriorated that authority had passed from the king's hands into those of Smendes and Tentamun, is a mystery. One is a little reminded of the state of affairs during the Second Intermediate Period when the Theban princes ruled in Upper Egypt and the Hyksos chieftains seized power in Lower Egypt. Probably Smendes rose to high authority by holding important administrative offices in the Delta under the king, and by marrying a Theban woman possibly related to the family of the high priests of Amun, or even to the royal family. Whatever the circumstances of his rise had been, there was clearly no doubt about his power when Wenamun came north. And indeed the position was soon regularised after the death of Ramesses XI, when Smendes became Pharaoh and the founder of the Twenty-first Dynasty in 1085 BC. The rulers of this dynasty established their capital at Tanis.

The whereabouts of Ramesses XI during this twilight time for the Twentieth Dynasty involves more than a question of residence. The two places where he most probably would have maintained his court were Memphis and Piramesse. Memphis, the earliest capital of the

A fractured granite obelisk lying in the temple area at Tanis inscribed with the names of King Ramesses II.

unified kingdom of Upper and Lower Egypt, remained an important city throughout Egyptian history. In the New Kingdom it was the administrative seat of the Lower Egyptian vizir, and a great commercial centre. There is no evidence, however, that it was ever the site of the royal residence during the Twentieth Dynasty. Piramesse was certainly a royal residence in the Twentieth Dynasty, and it is here that Ramesses XI would most probably have spent his time.

Unfortunately, the exact position of Piramesse in the eastern Delta has never been determined to the satisfaction of all scholars. By far the biggest ancient site in the area is the great mound of San el-Hagar, which was identified as Tanis by the French scholars who were the first to examine it during the Napoleonic invasion of Egypt in 1798. During the nineteenth century excavations appeared to produce evidence that suggested that Tanis and Piramesse were one and the same place. What was more, it emerged that Piramesse had itself been founded on the site of Avaris, the ancient capital city of the Hyksos.

What sort of place is this great ruin which may have been Avaris, then Piramesse, then Tanis? Today the whole district in which the mound of San el-Hagar stands is a dreary waste. It is situated a few miles to the south of Lake Menzala, a land-locked lagoon which lies between the north-eastern edge of the Delta and the Mediterranean Sea. All around the mound the country lies desolate, made barren by salt. It supports very little life by agriculture, and it is hard to believe that the city could ever have been surrounded by well cultivated fields. As an important port for the trade to Syria, it would not have suffered from having such a situation. But could the region ever have deserved the praise written about Piramesse in the New Kingdom?

When Auguste Mariette conducted the first excavation of any size on the site from 1860, he turned up great quantities of sculpture from what was undoubtedly a temple area. Many of the largest of the statues and much of the temple structure seemed to belong to Ramesses II; other sculptures belonged to earlier reigns, in particular to those of certain kings of the Twelfth Dynasty. Mariette also found strange sphinxes which were unlike any previously found. Their strangeness could only be attributed, so it was felt, to foreign influence, and for many years they were known as Hyksos sphinxes. Almost every new object dug up at Tanis raised a new problem. The sculptures in particular belonged to all periods from the Middle Kingdom to at least the Twenty-first Dynasty (from about 1900 BC to 1100 BC). What could be observed, however, was that on most of them the names of the kings for whom they were originally made had been erased, and those of New Kingdom kings substituted. Of the names which replaced the originals, the most common was that of Ramesses II. The conclusions to be drawn from Mariette's work were that the temple was probably a foundation of Ramesses II, possibly on the site of earlier sanctuaries, and that the place had been important in the days of the Hyksos.

Mariette was followed in 1884 by Flinders Petrie, and it was at Tanis that the unconventional Englishman conducted his first major piece of excavation. His eminent predecessor had only scratched the area of the whole site, and Petrie was not at all deterred from including among his priorities the task of 'tidying up' what Mariette had left unfinished. So apart from making explorations in the great mound which comprised the successive layers of occupation of the inhabited town right down to the late Roman Period (fourth century AD), he set about further work in the temple area, in particular making a plan of everything found by Mariette and himself. He made a much more systematic examination of the remains, including fragments of sculpture, and his most remarkable results were obtained from a study of the surviving pieces of a standing colossus of a king made of granite. According to Petrie's estimate, the figure when complete must have stood about ninety-two feet high, and weighed all of nine hundred tons. The nearest granite quarry was nearly six hundred miles away.

As far as the debate about the identification of Tanis with Piramesse was concerned, Petrie's excavation did not advance the solution very much. It still seemed that Ramesses II, who had left his mark as a builder at most places of importance in Egypt, had also been the greatest builder at Tanis. One thing about Egyptian kings which we have not properly considered, however, although it has been touched on, is their habit of usurping the works of their predecessors. In the case of Tanis this practice assumes very large proportions. On examination, scarcely anything at Tanis seems to have remained in its original state. Practically every piece of sculpture had been usurped once, twice, or even three times. To sort out the history of the site seems impossible. But one thing is certain: all the stone used at Tanis had to be brought from far away, and it is evident that some of the statues were brought to the Delta from places like Memphis, ready made. It suggests a desire to furnish a new site with undue haste. Was it even possible that there had been two moves, the first to Ramesses II's new town of Piramesse, and the second from there to the new capital of the Twenty-first Dynasty at Tanis?

Some hope of a solution seemed possible when the French archaeologist, Pierre Montet, started regular work at Tanis in 1929. The campaign he then began continued right up to the outbreak of the Second World War, was resumed after the war, and continues to this day, although Montet himself died in 1966. When he began his work there he had several intentions in mind: to prove beyond doubt that Tanis was the site of Avaris and Piramesse, and to discover material remains and documents which might throw light on the sojourn of the Children of Israel in Egypt and on their Exodus from Egypt. Montet approached his excavations with the mind more of an arm-chair scholar than a field archaeologist; but he had excavated extensively elsewhere and possessed great courage and determination. In consequence his work was not distinguished by the inspiration of a Petrie, or the punctiliousness of a Reisner or a Carter; it resembled in some respects the work of a scholar thumbing through the books in a library, making use of what he finds to write interpretative articles and studies. However, in Montet's case the statues and architectural fragments which littered the site at Tanis took the place of the books; and the evidence he collected from his siftings and digging was capable of very varied interpretation.

As far as his principal intentions were concerned, Montet cannot be said to have contributed very much towards the solution of problems. In a sense he helped, through his discoveries, to confuse

The top of the tomb of Psusennes at Tanis just after its discovery by Montet.

issues even further. After many years of very fruitful excavation he left the questions very much as he formulated them when he began work. It was not his fault that this was so; it was the fault, if this word can be applied to things, of the objects he found. Wherever he dug he found that the structures he unearthed contained such a jumble of material, in particular reused blocks of stone of many periods, that it was scarcely possible to construct a lucid history of Tanis.

Few excavations, however, are without their compensations, and in Montet's case his compensation was an extraordinary and unexpected find. In 1939 his work gang were engaged in clearing an area just outside the south-west corner of the great temple. It lay between the site of the first great pylon (gateway) which gave access to the first court of the temple, and the vast brick wall which enclosed the whole temple precinct. In this space there were great accumulations of apparent debris at the top of which were extensive remains of brick structures which could be dated to the last years of the Pharaonic Period. The site looked unattractive, and had been passed over when earlier excavators had placed their gangs to work in this neighbourhood. Montet, however, was not in a hurry to obtain results; he could afford the time to look at what others had ignored. So he decided at this time to tidy up the south-west corner of the temple precinct. The brick structures seemed to be chapels of some kind, but they also included what appeared to be an artist's workshop, containing unfinished sculptures. The workmen cleared away several layers of buildings and then, to the utter astonishment of all, at a level below that of the temple precinct they came upon the limestone roof of a small but solidly built chamber.

In such a position, just outside the main entrance of the temple, you would not expect to find a building of much importance; possibly a small shrine, or store chambers of a later date. You would certainly not expect to find a royal tomb in such a place. But that is what had been found. And, as it eventually became clear, it was not just one tomb, but a clutch of six, perhaps not all royal, but all belonging to very important people who had lived during the Twenty-first and Twenty-second Dynasties (1085–730 BC). The first structure to be entered was, to begin with, rather disappointing. A division had been made in the entrance chamber and one part was practically empty while the other contained a granite sarcophagus hewn out of what was probably a monument of Ramesses II; it held just a few bones. A small doorway, once blocked by a granite plug, led into a second chamber which had at some time been very thoroughly plundered. It still contained a few remains of burial equipment including some funerary figures, called ushabtis, inscribed with the name of a king called Sheshonq. A third chamber contained a rectangular coffin of sandstone which, from inscriptions, was identified as having held the body of King Takelothis II of the Twenty-second Dynasty (837–813 BC). The burial had been plundered, but there were enough fragments of gold jewellery and mummy equipment to show that the royal body had been quite well fitted out when it was placed in its coffin.

A fourth chamber completed this remarkable tomb. It consisted of a granite room surrounded by limestone, and it contained two sarcophagi. One was huge and made of granite; it had been made for the burial of King Osorkon II (860–837 BC), but had been fairly comprehensively plundered. Again, however, a few small objects had survived to provide hints of jewellery and other ornaments which had originally been included in the burial. Also the four Canopic jars of the king had survived. These were the receptacles in which the royal internal organs were placed. The second sarcophagus,

Bronze ushabti figure
from the tomb of
King Psusennes.

made of granite with a lid of sandstone, had held the mummy of the
prince Hornakhte, son of Osorkon II. The robbers of antiquity had
been content to make a hole in it through which they had been able
to remove some of the contents. But much had been left behind, and
from the fragments Montet could see that Hornakhte's mummy had
been placed in a gilded coffin within an outer silver coffin. Only
fragments of the coffins survived, but from the debris in the sarcophagus a very large number of objects were retrieved. They included
gold jewellery, divine figures and amulets of gold and semi-precious
stones, and mummy accoutrements of gold, such as the gold sheaths
placed on the fingers and toes of the body.

The contents of this first tomb were a strange mixture. The tomb
itself had without a doubt been made in the first instance for Osorkon
II and his son Hornakhte, who could only have been about twelve
years old when he died. The three first chambers were intended for
funerary furniture, but had been used for the reburials of other kings
like Takelothis II, and probably Sheshonq, after their own tombs
had been found violated in antiquity. As a structure the tomb was a
miserable affair; it was built only just below the surface because the
sub-soil water at Tanis would quickly have destroyed a burial made
well below ground level. As a 'house of eternity' it compared very
unfavourably with the royal tombs at Thebes. Yet it was evident
from the objects discovered that the bodies of the kings and of
members of their families were at that time prepared with a lavish-
ness of ornament which might almost rival what had been found on
Tutankhamun's mummy. On the other hand, the stone sarcophagi
used for these carefully prepared mummies were, in some cases at
least, improvised from other material and not at all well made.

Nevertheless, Pierre Montet had found a royal tomb in quite
unexpected circumstances, and his remarkable discovery was not to
end there. In all, he found six tombs in the group. Of these four had
been badly robbed. One had undoubtedly been made for Amenemope,
fourth king of the Twenty-first Dynasty, and another for Sheshonq
III of the Twenty-second Dynasty, whose violated body was probably moved into the tomb of Osorkon II, where it had again been
violated. The sixth tomb (actually the third in Montet's order of
discovery) turned out to be unrobbed, and it provided the greatest
thrills of the excavation. Like the first tomb it consisted of a limestone
structure containing one preliminary room and a granite-lined burial
chamber. Again the tomb had been intended for a double burial, and
the burial chamber was subdivided to receive two sarcophagi.

Furthermore the limestone mass of the structure contained two additional burial chambers which could only be reached by the removal of some of the limestone roofing slabs.

From the inscriptions on the walls it was clear that the tomb had been built for Psusennes, the third king of the Twenty-first Dynasty, who may have died in about 1010 BC. But like the first tomb opened by Montet, Psusennes' tomb had become the resting place for others after their own tombs had been robbed. In this new sepulchre they remained undisturbed until their modern discovery. The preliminary room, or ante-chamber, contained three burials, the most striking of which belonged to another king called Osorkon, otherwise not known, but presumably of the Twenty-second Dynasty. His mummy was in a gilded coffin within a silver coffin, the head of which was in the form of a falcon. The body and much of the inner coffin were almost completely rotted through the effects of damp. But again the excavators were able to recover much jewellery and a solid gold mask which covered the mummy's face. The other two burials were in very poor condition, having been badly affected by damp. Nevertheless the antechamber as a whole yielded a large quantity of funerary equipment including ten Canopic jars. Of the two burial chambers in the limestone mass of the tomb, one had originally held the body of a prince, Ankhefenmut; but for some reason his burial had been removed and his name hacked out from the inscriptions on the walls of the chamber. The second contained the intact burial of a Chief of Bowmen, Wendjebauendjed. An usurped sarcophagus of granite, made originally for a Theban priestly official, contained the body of Wendjebauendjed; he too had a gilded wooden coffin and a silver coffin, and his body was richly decorated with objects of gold and silver. Furthermore, he was buried with some fine gold and silver vessels, some of which appeared to be of earlier date; he seems to have taken the family plate with him to use in his after-life.

The two sections of the granite burial chamber contained the most exciting discoveries of all. In one was the original occupant of the tomb, Psusennes himself. Here was an undisturbed royal burial of the Twenty-first Dynasty, and what a mixture of splendour and the makeshift it was! The mummy was wonderfully equipped with the necessary jewellery and other accoutrements, and fitted with a splendid mask which falls little short of that found on the mummy of Tutankhamun. The inner coffin was silver, the outer of black granite, while the sarcophagus of pink granite had originally been

Golden goblet in the form of a lotus flower from the tomb of Psusennes

made for Merenptah, the successor of Ramesses II, whose tomb was at Thebes. Psusennes' funerary equipment also contained fine vessels of gold and silver, Canopic jars and ushabti figures; but the splendid furniture of earlier periods was missing, possibly because, since it was known that in the damp conditions of the Delta perishable materials would soon disintegrate, the practice had been abandoned at Tanis by this time.

Gold armlet decorated with the figure of a winged beetle from the tomb of Psusennes

In the second section of the burial chamber lay the mummy of the king Amenemope, moved there from his original tomb which Montet found robbed nearby. The mummy was placed in a wooden coffin within a large stone sarcophagus which had originally been prepared for Queen Mutnodjme, a wife of Smendes and mother of Psusennes. The tomb of Psusennes had surely been planned as a double tomb for the king and his mother. We are unlikely ever to know how the mummy of Amenemope came to occupy the second sarcophagus. Was Mutnodjme ever buried there? If so, why was she turned out to make way for Amenemope?

These last are just minor questions compared with the others posed by the remains of antiquity found at Tanis. The unexplored part of the site remains huge—far greater than the area already excavated. Future work may produce solutions for some of the problems, but it can be assumed that yet more problems will be raised. The discovery of the royal tombs was unexpected and thrilling. The evidence they provided of the decline in royal status was clear and sad. There may be more royal tombs, the tombs of royal officials, perhaps a palace, more temples and other public buildings, even traces of the port from which Wenamun set sail for Syria. The possibilities seem endless. What may be predicted, however, is that future discoveries will not conform with present expectations. The lottery of excavation will see to that.

10

The Sacred
Bulls of Memphis

In the autumn of 1850 a young Frenchman, Auguste Mariette, arrived in Egypt sent on a mission by the French Government to make a survey of the ancient manuscripts still preserved in the various Christian monasteries of the country. Christians in Egypt are called Copts, and their language, no longer spoken but still used in their churches, is Coptic. It is the direct descendant of the language of ancient Egypt, and in its written form it uses the Greek alphabet with a few additional letters derived from Egyptian hieroglyphics. The monasteries of Egypt had been the happy hunting grounds of several European manuscript collectors in the early nineteenth century, and large quantities of precious Coptic documents had been removed to European museums and libraries. In many cases the early collectors had not been too scrupulous in the methods they used to extract the manuscripts, and the monks and high officials of the Coptic Church had become very wary of allowing anyone to enter the monasteries to examine what might be left.

Mariette, at that time a young man of twenty-nine, held a junior post in the Louvre Museum in Paris. He had already developed a passion for Egyptology, but had not had much opportunity to follow his interests. The chance of a visit to Egypt was not to be missed, but the principal purpose of the visit had not fired him with much enthusiasm. Still, he tried his best, first in Alexandria and then in Cairo, to get official permission to visit the monasteries in the desert valley called the Wadi Natrun. He met with blank refusals. His protestations that he only wanted to make a record of the surviving documents, not to carry any of them away, were of

The Step Pyramid at Saqqara.

no avail. His mission was a failure. So, the day after he received his final refusal, he went up at evening time to the Citadel of Cairo from where a wonderful view of the city could be obtained. He marvelled at what he saw, and his eyes passed over the city to the distant line of the desert where something could still be seen in the evening haze of the pyramids of Giza. On the spur of the moment Mariette decided to make a visit to the pyramids, and on the following day he equipped himself with camping gear and stores and set off. After spending a week at Giza he moved south to Saqqara, the site of the great necropolis of Memphis, dominated by the Step Pyramid.

Here Mariette began a careful survey of the visible monuments, and in the course of his work he came across a limestone sphinx three-quarters buried in the sand. He saw at once that it was similar to several other sphinxes he had seen in Alexandria. They had been purchased from a Cairo dealer who claimed that they came from Saqqara where they had formed part of an avenue of sphinxes leading westwards into the desert. At the moment when he saw the buried sphinx, Mariette was reminded, so he claimed afterwards, of a passage in the *Geography* of Strabo, in which the Greek writer spoke of a temple of Serapis in a place near Memphis, much sanded up in his day (the early first century AD), approached by a way lined with sphinxes. It seemed to Mariette that Strabo had written his remarks almost to serve as a guide for future explorers. He felt sure that he had found the place described by Strabo, and his supposition was further confirmed by the discovery of an Egyptian inscription containing an invocation of Osiris-Apis, a god of dual nature, who could be equated with Serapis, a divine name occurring in Greek texts.

Excited by his deductions, and sure that he was on the threshold of a great discovery, Mariette decided to abandon his mission and to embark on an excavation with the funds at his disposal. It was a rash move for a young man of no reputation to take. Happily his judgement in this case was sound. With a small band of workmen he started to dig by the one visible sphinx. By a certain amount of trial and error the next sphinx was found, wholly buried in the sand, and from the distance separating the two it became possible to predict the positions of other sphinxes. The work proceeded quickly, moving from sphinx to sphinx. The avenue followed a relatively straight course for some hundreds of yards, and then turned sharply to the left, leading to the front of a small temple before which was ranged a remarkable semicircle of statues of Greek poets and philosophers. The temple had been built by Nectanebos of the Thirtieth Dynasty, the last Egyptian king (360–343 BC), and its remains bore many references to Osiris-Apis. Mariette thought that he had already found the Serapeum, the tomb of the sacred Apis bulls, or at least the temple closely connected with the tomb. In the immediate neighbourhood he could find nothing, and it was to be some months, and after much trouble from illness and interfering officials before ultimate success would come.

What was the Serapeum? Who was Serapis? Who were Apis and Osiris-Apis? Let us start with Apis. From the time of the First Dynasty the Apis was worshipped at Memphis in the form of a bull. He was a symbol of divine strength and fertility and his cult was closely connected with that of the king. In the manner of Egyptian gods he developed other characteristics and, as time passed, he became associated both with the sun god Re and with Ptah, the great creator god whose principal temple was at Memphis. The Apis was recognised by the markings on its body, and as soon as one died a search began for its successor—a bull-calf with similar markings. When it was found it was brought in triumph to Memphis where it was installed in special quarters built close to the temple of Ptah. The calf's mother, now recognised as a divine cow, was also established in honour at Memphis.

Limestone statue of the Greek poet Pindar, one of the figures found by Mariette at the temple in front of the Serapeum at Saqqara.

By the New Kingdom, and possibly much earlier, the Apis became almost as important in death as it had been in life. Like a dead person it became identified in death with Osiris, the god of the dead, and was invoked as the Osiris-Apis. Its death was mourned like the death of a king, and the funeral preparations and ceremonies were immensely elaborate. Before Mariette's discoveries it was already known that the Apis had been buried in a specially prepared tomb in the Memphite necropolis, but scarcely anything was understood of what went on at the time of burial, or of the nature of the burial itself.

As for Serapis, he was an entirely new god introduced into the company of Egyptian gods during the reign of Ptolemy I (304–282 BC), at the time when rule in Egypt had been taken over by

Macedonian Greeks. It is difficult now to discover exactly how Serapis developed, but it is generally agreed that in name he was derived from the Osiris-Apis of the last dynasties of Pharaonic Egypt. His cult was almost 'invented' to act as a religious link between the native Egyptians and the immigrant Greeks who had flooded into Egypt in the wake of Alexander the Great's invasion. In representation Serapis was human in form with a bearded face and a head topped by a box-like object called a *modius*. This was a corn-measure, and it signified the abundance of harvest. Serapis was particularly a god of the underworld, and embodied the characteristics of Osiris, on the Egyptian side, and of Zeus, the father of the gods, on the Greek side. A great temple of his cult was built in Alexandria, and this was called the Serapeum. What Strabo had described as the temple of Serapis at Saqqara was in reality a temple of Osiris-Apis, and it served as the mortuary temple for the cult of the dead Apis bulls. It was built before the establishment of the worship of Serapis, and should not therefore be called a Serapeum.

The remains of the Temple of Ptah at Memphis where the Apis bull had his quarters.

Some wrong names, however, stick, and it would now be impossible to think of Saqqara without a Serapeum. But the name

OPPOSITE
The gold mask of
King Tutankhamun

actually is applied today, as it was by Mariette, not to the temple of Nectanebos, which was found at the end of the avenue of sphinxes, but to the subterranean burial galleries, or catacomb, which Mariette discovered later. He knew from Strabo's account that the catacomb of the Apis bulls was to be found in the same area, and from observation of the ground to the west of the temple of Nectanebos, he could see roughly the line he ought to follow to reach it. So he set his men to work in several places in the hope of striking the entrance. Vast quantities of blown sand made the work difficult and slow. Shortage of money prevented the employment of more workmen. But this preparatory work was not wholly without profit, for in the course of clearing the mounds of sand, other structures were discovered, including important tombs of the Old Kingdom, some of which contained fine sculptures. Caches of votive bronzes and other small antiquities were also turned up and their discovery caused much interest among the antiquities dealers in Cairo. Unwelcome visitors on the excavation became frequent and gave Mariette much trouble. But he suffered his worst trouble on June 5 1851, when agents of the Khedive, the ruler of Egypt, came to Saqqara to shut down the dig and confiscate what had been found. Mariette had been digging without proper permission, and he might have expected such an abrupt intervention at some time.

In the course of the summer and autumn of 1851 matters were slowly settled. Not only was Mariette allowed to continue work, though under conditions that were not exactly to his liking, but he received a substantial grant of money from the French Government. The money was specially welcome because it meant that he could work, and also that his improper use of funds for other purposes had been overlooked. By November he had a small picked team working to the west of the temple on what was undoubtedly a man-made cutting in the desert rock. It was difficult making a clearance to the bottom because as the sand was removed, more from the surrounding mounds slipped down into the excavation. At last on November 12, a large, blocked, limestone door was discovered. Here without doubt was the entry to the tombs of the Apis bulls.

What Mariette had found was a catacomb for Apis burials used during the late dynasties and the Ptolemaic Period. There were long vaulted corridors off which opened the vaults of the individual burials. Each Apis was provided with a vast stone sarcophagus covered with a massive lid. The whole complex had, unfortunately,

been so pillaged through the centuries that scarcely anything remained to indicate the nature of the burials and the scale of decoration used on the bull mummies. The main gallery of this late Serapeum was 1150 feet long, and it contained twenty-four burials originally. Twenty sarcophagi were still in position in their vaults; their average weight has been estimated at sixty-five tons. Few of the sarcophagi were inscribed, but information about the dates of many burials was to be found in the small votive stelae which favoured people had been allowed to place in or near the vaults of the Apis who died in their lifetimes. The texts on these stelae included prayers addressed to the Apis for the benefit of the people who set them up. Working in the catacomb presented great problems; the debris from destruction by plunderers had been augmented by falls of rock from the roof; the air was bad, and the candles used by the explorers stayed alight only with difficulty; sand and dust lay thick everywhere. Even today a visit to the Serapeum in the train of a party of tourists can be like a walk through an old-fashioned London fog. The dust of ages, fine and all-penetrating, increases the eeriness inseparable from a place so associated with death and burial, though electric light has long replaced the candles of Mariette's day.

The discovery of the so-called greater vaults was followed by that of the lesser vaults, used from the mid-Nineteenth Dynasty down to the Twenty-sixth Dynasty, and then by some individual burials of the Eighteenth and Nineteenth Dynasties. Among the last Mariette found an intact tomb, holding two Apis burials made in the reign of Ramesses II. On March 19 1852 he entered the chamber and found two great wooden sarcophagi, one of which was accompanied by four large Canopic jars for the internal organs of the mummified Apis. There were large numbers of funerary statuettes in stone and faience, and other objects, many of which were inscribed with the name of Khaemwese, the eldest son of Ramesses II. The sarcophagi did not hold proper bull mummies, but collections of bones and other animal material in a poor state of preservation, mixed up with a quantity of funerary statuettes, fragments of gold and gold ornaments; again the name of Khaemwese occurred on many of the objects.

In all Mariette estimated that he recovered about seven thousand objects in the course of his excavation of the Serapeum. It is often considered as the first true excavation of modern times in Egypt, and its triumphant success was due directly to the acumen, know-

Above The scene on the back panel of the golden throne of Tutankhamun. The seated king is anointed with ointment by his wife.
Below Tutankhamun in his chariot attacks his Libyan enemies. A scene on the painted box of the king.

Alabaster slab used in the embalming ceremonies of the Apis bulls in the Temple of Ptah at Memphis.

ledge and determination of the excavator. Within a month of his arrival in Egypt for the first time, he had identified his site and begun his work. He knew nothing of excavation, but he understood much of what would now be considered basic excavator's knowledge. However, although he kept a reasonable record of his general activities, Mariette did not compile a detailed account of what he found. Subsequently he became so busy organising the new Antiquities Service, and in conducting operations in other parts of Egypt, that he never made a proper publication of his Serapeum finds. In that respect Mariette did not fulfil his obligation to scholarship; unhappily he was only the first of many excavators whose work was never properly completed by the publication of their results. It is a sad thing for archaeology in general that the thrill of excavation in the field is rarely matched by an enthusiasm for the working-up of results in the study.

Mariette's concern with the Serapeum lasted only a few years; but interest in it and in other aspects of the cult of the Apis bull have been much stimulated in recent times by other discoveries. One which provides some information about the life of the Apis before its death and mummification was made in Memphis in 1941 by the Egyptian archaeologists Ahmed Badawy and Mustafa el-Amir. Working a little to the south-east of the great temple of Ptah they uncovered a number of objects connected both with the living Apis and with the dead Apis. Among their finds were several alabaster slabs in the form of great beds, alabaster altars, and stone basins for the catching of liquids running off the alabaster slabs. There were also ox-bones, a jar with material from the mummification process, and two limestone reliefs showing mummified Apis bulls being transported in wheeled cars. Most of the dated objects could be assigned to the Twenty-sixth Dynasty. Here without a doubt was part of the area devoted to the Apis bull during its life, and the place where some of the mummification processes of the dead Apis were carried on after its death.

What emerged from these finds at Memphis provided some confirmation of a view earlier expressed by archaeologists who had worked on the site of another series of bull burials at Armant south of Thebes. Apparently the full mummification of the dead Apis only took place from the Twenty-sixth Dynasty onwards. From that time dated the greater vaults at Saqqara, where the burials were made in the great stone sarcophagi. From an examination of very ancient texts it seemed probable that in the Old Kingdom, and perhaps as late as the early New Kingdom, the Apis at death was partly eaten by the reigning king. This ritual feast might have been one of the acts performed by the living king to rejuvenate himself by absorbing the power and vitality of the divine bull. During the New Kingdom, however, for reasons which are no longer apparent,

Two limestone reliefs from Memphis in which mummified Apis bulls are shown being conveyed to their tombs on wheeled carts

more importance was placed on the burial and posthumous existence of the Apis. The earliest Apis tombs so far discovered belong to the Eighteenth Dynasty, and they may in fact represent the first formal burials. What Mariette found in his unrobbed burials of the reign of Ramesses II were not proper mummies, but kinds of carefully assembled bundles of animal material, perhaps the remains after the royal ritual meal. In neither of the sarcophagi did he find a bull's head, which struck him as being very strange.

By the Twenty-sixth Dynasty the Apis cult had changed its character somewhat and was not so private. According to Greek writers it was possible at certain times for the public to view the Apis as it was exercised in its enclosure. Herodotus describes the way it was looked after by a special staff, fed with fine food, and constantly groomed. It was at this time that proper mummification was employed for the dead Apis, and it may be assumed that the actual Apis was not eaten by the king. Perhaps a substitute was eaten in place of the divine bull. There is still, however, much to be learned about the details of the cult. For example, it is not certain whether the Apis in early times was actually slaughtered before he grew old, so that his powers in full strength might pass to the king. In later times, from inscriptions it looks as if the Apis was allowed to die a natural death.

Some of the inscriptions found by Mariette have only recently been published, and many facts about the Apis are only now being made known. During the Late Period, when an Apis died the clergy of the temple of Ptah at Memphis assumed control of the arrangements to be made. One of the first things that had to be done was to send a messenger throughout Egypt to collect donations to help pay for the burial. Meanwhile the body was taken from its quarters to the Chamber of Purification. Here the process of embalming took place. From the evidence dug up by the temple of Ptah, it seems that the Chamber of Purification lay close to, perhaps was even an extension of, the bull's quarters. The alabaster slabs and basins discovered in 1941 surely formed part of the equipment used in the preparation of the body. A space of seventy days was allowed for this preparation, and it was accompanied by vigils and fasts, prayers and lamentations. When the body was ready it was taken to Saqqara by a car of the kind shown on the slabs found at Memphis. At Saqqara the final rites were carried out including a sacred dance and the ceremonial opening of the mouth of the bull so that it could consume its food offerings after death.

Model mummy of an Apis bull or its mother found at Saqqara by W. B. Emery.

At the time of burial favoured officials were able to include their votive stelae in the vaults along with the new Apis mummy. Then the Serapeum was closed again to await the burial of the next Apis.

The bull-cult of Armant had as its object of devotion the bull known as Buchis. When the burials of the Buchis bulls were discovered in 1927 the excavators also found the graves of their cow mothers. At Saqqara, however, very few traces had ever been found of the mothers of the Apis bulls, although it was well known that these cows were honoured along with their divine sons, and were identified with the divine mother-goddess Isis. About half a mile to the north of the Serapeum lies an area of the Saqqara necropolis occupied by tombs of the earliest dynasties. Here in the years before the war, and after the war up to 1956, the British archaeologist W. B. Emery excavated many First Dynasty tombs. When he returned to work at Saqqara in 1964 he concentrated on another part of the same area. Here he uncovered tombs of the Third Dynasty and a series of catacombs devoted to various animal cults—ibises, baboons, falcons. In 1968 in the course of clearing mounds of debris, Emery came across large quantities of cow bones, considerable remains of wooden furniture, some of it gilded, and sledges of a kind used to drag heavy burials. He also uncovered many simple cow and bull burials, and a model bull or cow mummy made of wood with a real skull forming the basis of the head. It was painted with distinctive Apis markings and seemed to represent the bull or its mother. Further, he found the remains of a small temple with dedications to the Apis and to Isis, 'mother of Apis'. Like the temple found before the Serapeum by Mariette, Emery's temple also had been built by Nectanebos, the last king of the Thirtieth Dynasty.

117

For Emery the discovery of so much material relating to the burials of the Apis and its mother was a case of a return to the past, for he had been largely responsible for the discovery of the burials of the Buchis bulls and their mothers at Armant in 1927. The presence of special tombs for the mothers of the sacred bulls at Armant suggested that similar special arrangements would have been made for the burials of the mothers of the Apis bulls at Saqqara. Now in 1968 Emery was convinced that a catacomb containing the cow burials of the mothers of Apis could not be far away. His belief was confirmed in 1970 when his workmen, digging in the rocky escarpment, a little distance to the east of the Nectanebos temple, discovered the 'Resting Place of Isis, Mother of the Apis'. Like the great Serapeum it consisted of an underground gallery with vaults opening off it to provide chambers for individual burials. Unhappily the condition of the catacomb was terrible. Not only had the burials been robbed and the great stone sarcophagi smashed, but much of the roof had collapsed, and the whole complex was silted up with sand. In the course of preliminary excavation and examination a number of votive stelae were found. Like those from the Serapeum, they provided useful information about the burials. The earliest date discovered was 393 BC, and the latest 41 BC. So far the catacomb has only been partially cleared, and it may be years before the whole is accessible. It is unlikely, however, that very much will be recovered to add to the story of the Apis and its mother. Yet it is in itself important to know where the cow burials were, and to realise that in kind they were scarcely inferior to those of the Apis bulls themselves.

So, by excavation, often over many years, the picture of one aspect of ancient Egyptian religious practices may be built up. The finds of one excavator will complement those of another; sometimes apparently contradictory results will be obtained. But in time, provided that the discoveries are well published, the parts will come together to form a whole. An excavator never knows how his finds may help in the interpretation of earlier discoveries. If he knows the work of his predecessors he will probably himself recognise the significance of his finds. If he is not well informed of earlier work, his own task will be the harder, and he may suffer the shame of having some study-bound scholar pointing out to him what he has missed. Emery at Saqqara knew what to expect, and therefore knew what to look for. Sadly he was not to reap the full rewards of his discovery, for he died in the spring of 1971.

11

The Decipherment
of Hieroglyphs

At the very beginning of this book mention was made of the
publication of a pamphlet by Jean-François Champollion, in which
he announced his discoveries concerning the decipherment of the
hieroglyphic script. The success of Champollion's system, which
was clearly founded on a proper understanding of some of the
principles on which the hieroglyphic script was based, led to the
translation of many Egyptian texts. As the years passed more texts
were discovered and translated, and knowledge about ancient
Egypt grew rapidly. We now know so much about the Egyptian
language that it is possible for a scholar to understand the greater
part of any new text almost at first sight. It is therefore difficult for
Egyptologists today to understand the state of utter ignorance in
which students of antiquity existed as far as ancient Egypt was
concerned in the years before Champollion's decipherment.

By the time of the Roman conquest of Egypt in 30 BC the hieroglyphic script was only used for religious inscriptions and small
votive stelae. Native Egyptian knowledge of hieroglyphics seems to
have died a lingering death during the centuries of Roman occupation. Few people could have understood texts written in hieroglyphs,
and their number diminished rapidly. By the end of the fourth
century AD hieroglyphs had become extinct as a means of communication. Greek was the official language of Egypt, and most writings
were composed either in Greek or in the vernacular Egyptian
language written in the new Coptic script. It is not surprising that
knowledge of the hieroglyphic script was lost at the time of its
disappearance as a medium of communication. What is surprising
is that no Greek scholar apparently made a study of hieroglyphs

before this moment came. The learned men who flocked to Alexandria to work in and around the great library established there in the Ptolemaic Period seemed quite content to concentrate on Greek literature and learning. If only some of them had looked beyond the hot-house confines of that ancient seat of learning and examined the language and writing of their Egyptian contemporaries in the rest of Egypt, perhaps ignorance of hieroglyphs would not have been so complete in the many centuries which followed.

Ivory tablet found in a tomb of the First Dynasty at Saqqara, dated to the reign of King Djet. An early example of the use of hierogylphics

Some interest was shown in hieroglyphs by certain late Greek writers, but their studies developed when it was too late for them to obtain real knowledge of how the script worked. The *Hieroglyphica* of Horapollo was a work which was much consulted by European scholars after its rediscovery in the fifteenth century AD. It was supposed to have been written by an Egyptian and translated into Greek, but its peculiar character suggests that it could not have been written by any Egyptian who really understood hieroglyphs. In all probability the work was composed by a Greek who pretended that it was of Egyptian origin in order to give his work a kind of authenticity. Horapollo's method was to take individual hieroglyphic signs and describe their meanings and the origin of their meanings. The explanations are mostly fanciful and full of vague philosophical ideas, but in some cases it is evident that the author was not wholly without knowledge. For example, he says that the hieroglyphic sign of the vulture meant 'mother', which is in fact true; he also says that it meant 'mother' because there were no male vultures, which is patently untrue.

Throughout late medieval times and in the subsequent centuries, attempts were made to assign meanings to hieroglyphs but in almost every case the enquirers were wildly wrong. They could not believe that the hieroglyphic script was just a means of writing. It had to be invested with mystery; hidden meanings were lurking behind every strange sign. The discovery of Horapollo's treatise only seemed to confirm this point of view. In the course of the eighteenth century interest in Egypt was stimulated greatly by the increasing ease with which European travellers found they could travel there. Accounts of these travels were published, and the general reading public became acquainted with the antiquities and monuments of a new and exotic culture. How much more interesting it all would be if someone could find the key to the hieroglyphs! At just this moment the discovery was made which led to the solution of this centuries-old puzzle.

In 1798 Napoleon invaded Egypt with a French force. His ultimate purpose was to make a strike at the British in India, but for the moment Egypt provided a sufficient objective. With his expedition he took a party of French scholars who were to make a complete record of all they might find in Egypt, of antiquity, geography, natural history, and so on. His campaign was extraordinarily successful, and he occupied the whole of the country. But he knew that he was vulnerable to attack from the sea, and took steps to establish sound bases and fortifications in the Delta. In 1799 a detachment of French troops, commanded by an officer named Bouchard, was working on the foundations of an extension to a fort near the town of Rashid (Rosetta) in the Western Delta. The pick of one of the soldiers struck a large slab of basalt (a hard, black rock), and he noticed that it had writings carved upon it. By some miracle of understanding the soldiers felt that the stone might be of some importance; they cleaned it up and sent it to General Menou, the commander in Alexandria. He in turn sent it to Cairo where it was handed over to the Institute set up by the team of scholars who had accompanied the expedition.

Looking back to that time, when most of Europe was involved in war, it is amazing to see how quickly knowledge of the Rosetta Stone, as it came to be called, spread among scholars. By simple inspection it could be seen that there were three sections to the inscriptions, each written in a different script. At the top was a hieroglyphic text, in the middle a text written in a cursive script, later to be called Demotic, and at the bottom a Greek text. It was assumed rightly from the start that the three sections probably represented three versions of the same text. Copies and casts were made and sent to Paris, and from there further copies were distributed. The stone itself was confiscated by the British forces after the surrender of the French in Egypt in 1801, and it was brought to London in 1802. From London copies were again distributed to British scholars and to learned societies throughout Europe. Such was the community of scholarship in those days that the barriers of war did not prevent free communication between scholars of hostile countries.

As the Greek language was well known it was immediately possible to discover what the part written in Greek was about. Happily this section was preserved on the stone almost completely, and although the language of the text was phrased in a strange legal Greek, unlike the Greek of classical Athens, its general mean-

The Rosetta Stone.

ing was clear. It contained the copy of a decree which had been passed by an assembly of Egyptian priests who met at Memphis in 196 BC. It honoured the king, Ptolemy V, named Epiphanes, and contained an enumeration of the many benefits he had conferred on Egyptian priests and temples. At the end of the text a final clause specified that the decree should be engraved in Greek and Egyptian and that copies should be set up in all the temples throughout Egypt. This clause therefore confirmed the suspicions of those who had first examined the stone that the three parts contained the same text written in three different scripts. Two were Egyptian and one was Greek. Here was what scholars had been waiting for—a bilingual text which would surely provide the key to open the door to the vast edifice of Egyptian written records.

The names of King Tutankhamun in hieroglyphics from a wooden chair in his tomb.

It is hard for us to imagine the excitement generated by the discovery of the Rosetta Stone. Scholars were waiting throughout Europe in their studies, like greyhounds in their traps, to receive their copies and to leap forward in the great decipherment stakes. It was a time of great claims and counter-claims; many had pre-conceived ideas to confirm; others were more scientific. As early as 1802 a Frenchman, Silvestre de Sacy, was in the field with a paper identifying correctly, but on the wrong basis (as we now know), some of the royal names in the Demotic text. On his heels came a Swedish scholar, named Åkerblad, who was not only a linguist but also a lover of puzzles; he had the knowledge and the inclination to tackle the problem. In a matter of weeks, and working from de Sacy's results, he succeeded in determining the alphabetic nature of some of the signs used in the royal names. He also identified the words for 'Greek', 'temple', 'love', 'Egyptian', and was able to confirm his identifications by comparing his results with the known Coptic equivalents for the same words. Coptic is the name used for the Egyptian language in its very last stage when it was used by the Christian inhabitants of Egypt in early medieval times; it was written in the Greek alphabet and was known to European scholars before hieroglyphics were deciphered. Åkerblad also prepared a kind of alphabet from the Demotic text and was correct in about half his values, as later discoveries showed.

The work of these earliest decipherers was concentrated on the

Demotic text because it was better preserved on the Stone than the hieroglyphic text. In consequence it was easier to find groups in it which could be seen apparently to correspond with words in the Greek text. The Demotic script was very cursive; it had developed from earlier hieratic, a cursive script itself which, as we have seen, bore the same kind of relationship to hieroglyphics as hand-writing does to printing. Hieratic as used by professional scribes writing on papyrus became more and more unrelated to hieroglyphics as time went on, and by the time it had developed into Demotic the relationship with hieroglyphics was too remote to be at all obvious. Demotic was, therefore, the successor of hieratic as the regular script used for writing on papyrus, for non-religious documents. The names given to these scripts are not strictly accurate, Demotic meaning 'popular' and hieratic 'priestly'; but time and usage have made them into technical terms in Egyptology. Today many Egyptologists find reading texts in Demotic very difficult, and specialist scholars devote much time to its particular study. It is amazing to us, therefore, to think that the earliest serious students of decipherment concentrated on the Demotic, not the hieroglyphic, text on the Rosetta Stone.

After a few years in which the wild speculations of enthusiasts and occultists provided the greatest activity in the field of decipherment, a very substantial advance was made along the right lines by an English scientist, Thomas Young. His attention was first stimulated in about 1814 when a friend of his asked him to study some fragments of papyrus brought back from Egypt. In a very short time Young made himself acquainted with the state of knowledge in the field of decipherment, and began to work on both the hieroglyphic and the Demotic texts on the Rosetta Stone.

Between 1814 and 1819 Young published a number of results obtained from his researches, not all of which were subsequently to be supported by the discoveries of Champollion. He produced what he described as translations of the hieroglyphic and Demotic

The first words of the Great Harris Papyrus written in the hieratic script with a hiero-glyphic transcription given below. It reads, from right to left: 'Regnal year 32, third month of summer, day 6, under the majesty of the King of Upper and Lower Egypt, Ramesses III. May he live, be prosperous and healthy.' In the original the unfilled signs of the hieratic text are written in red ink.

Jean-François
Champollion by Leon
Cogniet.

sections of the Rosetta Stone, succeeded in equating groups in both texts, and proved that the groups of signs contained within oval rings in the hieroglyphic text constituted royal names. This last idea had been put forward earlier, but Young was the first to establish its validity. He was able to show not only that the name Ptolemy occurred on the Rosetta Stone in such an oval, but that the same name and that of Cleopatra, also in an oval, were to be found on an obelisk which had been found at Philae in Upper Egypt. This obelisk was brought back to England in 1819 by W. J. Bankes, its discoverer, who set it up in his park in Dorset where it stands to this day. Young also determined the meanings of many groups of signs in the hieroglyphic and Demotic parts of the Rosetta Stone, but he was unsuccessful in applying phonetic values to signs. He did, however, recognise that the Demotic part and the hieroglyphic part conveyed the same basic text, and that the actual forms of Demotic signs were derived from hieroglyphic originals.

Important though Young's discoveries were, they did not advance full understanding of Egyptian hieroglyphics beyond a certain point. Although he could recognise words and spell out proper names, he could not read a text, assign values to groups or elucidate the grammar of the language which lay behind the strange writing. Nevertheless his published results were seen by a young Frenchman who had devoted himself heart and soul to decipherment from a very early age. He must have derived some insight into certain problems from Young's discoveries, but it would be wrong to overestimate his debt to Young, or to claim that Young was truly the first decipherer of hieroglyphs. That title must go to the man who first was able to take an Egyptian text, for which no Greek parallel existed, and make a translation in which the meanings of the words and the grammar of the language equally contributed to the result. The title of first decipherer must go to Jean François Champollion.

Born in the town of Figeac in Southern France in 1790, Champollion showed signs of genius at a very early age. He received his earliest education from his elder brother, Jacques Joseph Champollion, and he soon showed a remarkable gift for languages. In addition to the classical languages, he mastered the rudiments of several oriental languages including Hebrew, Arabic and Coptic. This solid linguistic foundation was to be of the greatest practical use when he came to study the form of the Egyptian language, for he already understood that not all languages followed the pattern of the classical and principal European languages. He even obtained some knowledge of Chinese. In 1801 he was sent to school in Grenoble, and it was in that town in the following year that he met Jean Baptiste Fourier, the local senior government official whose secretary Jacques Joseph Champollion had become. Fourier, a mathematician, had been in Egypt as one of the scholars who set up the Institute in Cairo. He had developed a lasting interest in the country and had made a small private collection of antiquities. Hearing of his secretary's precocious younger brother, he invited him to visit him, and he told the boy much about Egypt and showed him his antiquities. The young Champollion was at that moment set upon his course for life, and he then determined to become the decipherer of hieroglyphs. This was in the year when the Rosetta Stone reached London from Egypt.

Throwing himself with all his enthusiasm into his new-found study Champollion worked constantly towards his determined goal. At the age of seventeen he published a grandiose plan for a work to be called *Egypt under the Pharaohs*, which was to be an encyclopaedia covering all aspects of ancient Egypt. He quickly compiled the first volume on the geography of Egypt, but it was not published for seven years, when it did not receive a very favourable reception. His single-minded determination and his tendency to use the discoveries of others without full acknowledgment, made him unpopular with scholars working in the same field. Also his political sympathies, freely expressed, were not altogether acceptable to the changed régime in France after the fall of Napoleon.

The basic problem which absorbed most of Champollion's energies was the precise nature of the hieroglyphic script. Was it truly alphabetic? One difficulty which he, like other early decipherers, found hard to overcome, was that in the case of some letters of the alphabet the Egyptians had more than one sign. Then again there were signs which seemed not to be of just one letter value. Other signs seemed to be without any value at all. One of the real handicaps which rendered the work of early Egyptologists particularly difficult was inherent in the Rosetta Stone itself. The hieroglyphs used in the first text on the stone were not very typical of Egyptian hieroglyphs of the earlier periods when the script was widely used throughout Egypt for all kinds of texts. In the Ptolemaic Period, when the Rosetta Stone was set up, hieroglyphs were only used for limited purposes. This text therefore was a most unsuitable beginner's piece for decipherment. Champollion was not unaware of this difficulty, and he was not at all sure that the results he achieved from his studies of the Rosetta Stone would be applicable to inscriptions of earlier periods. Not until he began to use the evidence of other texts did he gain confidence in his methods, and it was not until 1822 that he felt so sure of his results that he could make a communication to the Academy of Inscriptions in Paris.

His announcement took the form of a letter to Monsieur Dacier, the Secretary of the Academy. It contained, in addition to an exposition of the principles on which Champollion's work was based, a list of the cartouches of Egyptian rulers (including Roman emperors) from Alexander the Great to Antoninus Pius, and an alphabet of hieroglyphs which was in essence wholly correct. He limited his published investigation to the hieroglyphs of the Ptolemaic and Roman Periods, but he declared his belief that his interpretation would be found to be applicable to hieroglyphs of earlier periods. So conclusive were his results, and so convincingly had he demonstrated them, that for most scholars interested in the Egyptian script there was no further room for argument.

Shortly after Champollion had made his epoch-making announcement in his *Lettre à Monsieur Dacier relative à l'alphabet*

Part of the Demotic text on the Rosetta Stone. It represents the italicised words in the following sentence: 'This decree shall be set up on a stela of hard stone in *sacred* (hieroglyphic), *and native* (Demotic) *and Greek letters.*'

OPPOSITE
Above The temple of
Isis at Philae partly
submerged by the lake
behind the first
Aswan Dam.
Below The recon-
struction of the temple
of Ramesses II at Abu
Simbel after it had
been raised above the
waters of the new
Lake Nasser. The
feet of two of the
great figures of the
king before the
temple can be seen.

des hiéroglyphes phonétiques (as the communication was called), he found on examining a royal cartouche copied from the temple of Ramesses II at Abu Simbel that he could decipher the name Ramesses. This discovery was soon followed by the decipherment of the cartouche of Tuthmosis, a name held by several Eighteenth Dynasty Pharaohs. In deciphering these cartouches he had clearly proved to his own satisfaction that his method worked for hieroglyphs of earlier times. When he realised what he had done he rushed to his brother Jacques Joseph, managed to say 'I've got the answer', and then fell into a state of collapse which lasted for five days.

Once the initial breakthrough had taken place progress was rapid and confident. Two years later Champollion published a much larger work on the system behind hieroglyphic writing. In the short space since his first announcement to the Academy he had greatly enlarged the range of his identifications and was able to offer translations of short phrases. His authority was now fully established, and through the patronage of royal and other backers he was able to travel to Egypt and to the places where Egyptian antiquities were gathered in Europe, to collect material and to further his researches. Unfortunately the strains of his life had been too great, and in 1832, at the early age of 42, he died. Much of his own work remained unpublished, but his brother devoted his life to seeing that nothing remained unavailable to scholars.

After Champollion's death other scholars continued and enlarged the scope of the study of hieroglyphics. In time it was appreciated that the script was much more complicated than any early scholar had thought. Some signs were indeed alphabetic, but others stood for two or even three letters; again there were signs which stood for whole words or indicated the meanings of words by representing appropriate visual images. Slowly the mysteries of the script were unravelled, but, looking back, as we now can in the certainty of knowledge, on the decipherment contest of one hundred and fifty years ago, it is clear that the debt owed by Egyptology to Champollion is immense. Although others achieved some of the results he incorporated in his work, his own success was inspired by a genius which transcended the ability of ordinary hard work. At some moment, by inspiration he was able to make the necessary mental leap which brought success. It cannot be doubted that in time hieroglyphs would have been deciphered by others, but Champollion's genius saved everyone time—perhaps decades.

12

The Silver Treasures of Barbarians

In antiquity the realm of Egypt—the two lands of Upper and Lower Egypt—was very precisely determined geographically. It included the cultivable land of the Nile Valley from the Delta in the north to the Island of Elephantine six hundred miles to the south. At Elephantine a change came over the nature of the river. Here the flow of water was broken up by a series of islands and rocky outcrops which produced violent rapids in time of flood and a difficult passage at low water. This part of the river is now known as the First Cataract of the Nile. Five more similar regions of rapids lie at irregular intervals further upstream almost as far as Khartoum in the Sudan. Although the Egyptians knew much of the region to the south of Elephantine, they remained content to consider Egypt's real southern boundary to lie at this place. It was as if Egypt's extent was fixed by divine ordinance. Her power could extend beyond her borders, but what lay beyond could never be regarded as part of what was known as the 'Beloved Land'.

According to Egyptian mythology, or at least one strain in its tangled web, the source of the Nile lay just to the south of Elephantine, where its flood was said to pour forth from a great cavern. The whole region of the First Cataract was invested with mystery and legend, and it always had a special religious character. Nevertheless, trade, national security, and natural curiosity drove the Egyptians from very early times to penetrate the lands to the south of Elephantine. At first little attempt was made to establish any permanent presence in the southern land, which came to be called Kush. From the time of the Middle Kingdom, however, settlements were built and fortresses placed at strategic positions to

Above Silver crown set with semi-precious stones from one of the royal burials at Ballana. *Below* The face of the silver coffin of King Psusennes from Tanis, *c* 1050 BC.

The First Cataract
region of the Nile at
Aswan.

guard the trade routes and to look out for hostile attacks. During the
New Kingdom the great kings of the Eighteenth and Nineteenth
Dynasties built temples in Kush in which they were themselves
worshipped as gods along with other, better qualified members of
the Egyptian company of gods. The most famous of these temples
was that made by Ramesses II at Abu Simbel, a remarkable rock-cut
sanctuary with four mighty seated colossi of the king dominating its
façade.

Further temples were built in the region south of Elephantine
during the Ptolemaic and Roman Periods, and the religious character
of Nubia (as the area is now called) persisted down to medieval
times. Christianity obtained a strong hold there, and the remains of
churches and monasteries could still be seen throughout the region
until a few years ago. Now most are submerged under the waters
of the new lake which has built up behind the High Dam constructed
a few miles to the south of Elephantine. This High Dam is the
second dam to have been built across the Nile south of Elephantine
in modern times. The first, known as the Aswan Dam after the
town of Aswan which lies on the east bank of the Nile opposite
Elephantine, was constructed between 1899 and 1902. It produced
a narrow lake which extended southwards for one hundred and
forty miles. Archaeologists were much worried at the effect that the
raising of the waters would have not only on the standing monuments

of Nubia, but also on unidentified town sites and cemeteries.

Between 1907 and 1911 the Aswan Dam was heightened by sixteen feet because the original dam was not able to do all that the irrigationists had hoped. On this occasion the archaeologists were ready, and the Egyptian Antiquities Service organised the First Archaeological Survey of Nubia to examine sites which might be submerged, and to record fully the scenes and inscriptions in temples which would be partially drowned. In this campaign the leading archaeologist to begin with was Reisner, the excavator of the tomb of Hetepheres. He uncovered many cemeteries in the region and, with his customary efficiency, analysed his finds and identified various stages of culture which could not be directly linked with contemporary Egyptian cultural periods. Among these stages A, B and C were early (from about 3200 BC down to about 1800 BC), and X was very late (third to seventh centuries AD). The First Archaeological Survey of Nubia lasted for four seasons and in that time not only were very many ancient sites excavated, but most of the temples of Nubia were recorded.

Unfortunately the demands made on the waters of the Nile were ever increasing as Egypt's population expanded, and it was not long after the First World War that it was again decided to raise the Aswan Dam. Once more the threat to ancient sites in Nubia was appreciated by the Antiquities Service, and a Second Archaeological Survey was planned. Sites to be flooded by the new rise in the waters were not thought to be as numerous as those affected by the first raising of the dam, so a somewhat smaller campaign was envisaged. To find a director who could manage a task of this kind, which involved distinct hardship in manner of life for many months each year, was not easy. In the end an unexpected, but inspired, choice was made. W. B. Emery was invited to tackle the job. It was 1929 and Emery was just twenty-six years old.

Emery's appointment at such an early age to this responsible and exacting post is in retrospect surprising. But at this time in Egypt it must have been already clear to those who understood the qualities needed by a field archaeologist that he was particularly gifted. He had first come to Egypt when he was only twenty-one to work for Robert Mond in his excavations in the Theban necropolis. By good fortune and natural flair Emery had a series of profitable seasons, and then in 1927 he had been sent by Mond to Armant where he discovered the burials of the Buchis bulls and of their mothers. This discovery, which was directly due to Emery's

Negroes carrying the exotic products of tropical Africa: giraffe tails, ebony, a leopard skin, a monkey and a baboon. From the tomb of Sobkhotpe at Thebes, *c* 1420 BC

131

skill in 'reading' the ground, made his reputation as a digger of more than usual talent. He was therefore well-equipped to be director of the Second Archaeological Survey of Nubia.

The prospect of three or four long seasons in Nubia was not, however, very attractive. To begin with, living conditions would be rather poor. There would be a house-boat or two to live and work in. In no place would they stay for more than a few days—just long enough to investigate the possibilities of a cemetery or town site; rarely would the results require a full-scale excavation and a long stay. It would be difficult to get supplies, and the heat would be intense. It would not be uncommon to meet temperatures up to 120°F at the beginnings and ends of seasons. However, Emery was young and enthusiastic, and he jumped at the chance of being able to range widely over ninety miles of little known country, his own master for most of the time.

Using methods of recording developed by Reisner during the First Archaeological Survey, Emery's expedition was able to make very steady progress, moving south from Aswan. He had in his team one British archaeologist, L. P. Kirwan, five Egyptian archaeologists, and one hundred and fifty Egyptian workmen, including a select band of Quftis, the specialist diggers first trained by Petrie. They travelled together like a nomadic tribe, pitching camp for a few days, investigating a district by foot, excavating a few tombs, and then packing up camp and moving on again. They carried all their supplies with them, including the special dried bread baked for the workmen by their wives before the season began—enough to last for several months. Working and living so closely together for long periods of time, they developed a community of purpose and communal spirit not often found on excavation teams. In consequence more work was accomplished in a short time than was commonly the case. Techniques were developed which were brought to a high pitch of efficiency. No time was wasted by travelling, everything needful had to be done on the spot, including the photography and treatment of objects recovered from the excavations.

By the end of the second season in the spring of 1931 it looked as if one more season would see the end of the campaign. Emery's team had reached Abu Simbel, nearly at the end of the stretch of the Nile Valley which was likely to be affected by the rise of the waters. At this place the team reassembled early in November 1931. As the Egyptian workmen had not yet arrived, Emery and his assistants did a survey on foot of the district to the south of Abu Simbel on the west bank of the river. It was known as Ballana, a sparsely populated scrubby region with a few palm trees and little apparently to interest the archaeologists. In the course of their reconnaissance they came across a number of hillocks dotted about the ground, partly concealed by shrubs. On casual inspection they looked natural, but when Emery climbed to the top of one he became convinced that they were not natural, but man-made. He was to discover later that the mounds had not passed unnoticed by earlier visitors to the region, but only some observers—and those not always the most experienced—had thought them to be tomb mounds.

This horse model wears the silver trappings from a burial at Qustol.

While the problem of the Ballana mounds was being weighed, news came that illicit excavators had been at work on the other side of the river at a place called Qustol. When Emery went to inspect the site he was surprised to find that the robbers had uncovered tombs of the people called X-group by Reisner, and that these tombs were in the neighbourhood of more mounds like those at Ballana. The dilemma in which Emery found himself was considerable. On the one hand it seemed wholly desirable, in fact essential, to investigate at least some of these mounds; on the other hand, it would take his team many weeks to move the large mounds, and the possible results were very uncertain. This was supposed to be his last season, and he had a fair deal of ground still to cover before he completed his Nubian survey. In addition, the money allocated to him by the Antiquities Service was running low, and it was by no means certain that he would be given any more if the work extended to another season. A further consideration was that the mounds lay at a level which would possibly not be reached by the waters of the raised Nile. So the decision to excavate involved the possibility of major folly. Happily Emery and his colleagues decided to make some trial investigations, and their expectations were not unjustified.

The first mound to be examined was at Qustol; it had been robbed and the excavators were able to follow the robbers' passage into the burial chamber where they found a mass of broken pottery, smashed wooden objects and many human bones. The robbers had got in by the back door, as it were, and Emery thought that it would be worth investigating the proper entrance which probably consisted of a descending ramp lying below the mound itself. Even though the burial were robbed it would be interesting to discover exactly what the form of the whole structure was like. On November 10 work began on an adjacent mound, slightly smaller than the first one examined. Starting on the west side, they made a large cutting into the tumulus. By the end of the month the head of a downward sloping ramp was reached. As the slope was followed a few metal objects were found, including a vicious-looking horse-bit which turned out to be made of silver. Soon a horse skeleton was found, followed by the skeletons of more animals, horses, donkeys and camels. At the bottom of the ramp in what looked like a small courtyard in front of the actual entrance to the tomb, the excavators found further horses. They had been killed in this very place, and were fully caparisoned with silver-

A bronze censer in
the form of a lion
from Ballana.

mounted saddles and other trappings of leather fitted out with
silver. Beside them were the skeletons of their grooms. It was
evident that the owner of the tomb had gone to his after-life well
provided with animals and with his special horses. From an examination of the skeletons it emerged that the animals had been pole-axed;
the skeletons of the grooms showed no signs of violence, and it was
concluded that they were probably poisoned.

The inside of the tomb itself produced further evidence of
human sacrifice. Again, however, the excavators were to find they
had been beaten in their search by robbers, and the chambers of
the tomb were in a state of complete confusion. In order to confirm
his belief that an intact mound would mean an intact approach
ramp, even if the actual burial had been breached by tunnelling
from outside the area of the mounds, Emery decided to examine
the ramp of the first tomb he had looked at. Here again on the
ramp an incredible jumble of animal remains was uncovered.
Horses, donkeys, camels, dogs and sheep lay in an almost in-
extricable mass, within which were large quantities of silver and
bronze trappings, the remains of leather saddles, embroidered
saddle cloths and dyed sheep-skin coverlets. At the bottom of the
ramp, in a rock-cut room leading off the forecourt of the burial

chamber, a further group of six horses was found undisturbed. These horses had been decked out with even more elaborate trappings—fine medallions embellished the head-stalls which were themselves composed of silver chains; the bits in the horses' mouths were also of silver, as were the reins and bridles. Heavy collars around their necks were fitted with silver medallions set with precious and semi-precious stones. In another rock-cut room on the other side of the forecourt lay the skeletons of fifty large dogs, two men and two more horses, not decked out like the others. Here surely was the tomb-owner's hunting pack with its keepers.

When these discoveries had been shown to the Director of the Antiquities Service, sufficient funds were made available for Emery to complete the work at Qustol and to cross the river to probe the mounds at Ballana. None of the remaining Qustol tombs yielded as much as the first two, but several of them produced surprises in the types and natures of objects found, often concealed haphazardly in the earth mounds themselves like currants in a cake, as Emery used to say. Some things were crude and barbarous; some objects bore decorations derived from ancient Egyptian art; other objects were clearly traceable to Greek sources.

To this day nobody has satisfactorily settled the question of who the X-group peoples were. They inhabited parts of Nubia between the third and the seventh centuries AD, but being illiterate, they have left no written records. Unlike the ancient Egyptians they believed in providing their chiefs with actual human servants for their after-life. The tombs contained abundant proof of rough and bloody practices. An excavator can feel reasonably attracted to the ancient Egyptians; the X-group people are singularly unattractive.

At Ballana the excavators started on a huge mound, eighty yards in diameter. To begin with Emery was not absolutely convinced that the mounds on this side of the river were the tumuli of tombs. For four weeks the gang toiled on the great mound cutting a section down to ground level. There was no sign of the brickwork which would have marked the roofing of the underground tomb-chambers. It looked very much as if four weeks had been wasted on what was a natural mound. Then one of the best of the Qufti workmen, who had gone on scraping away in his own corner came upon a few pieces of pottery. What a relief these provided! They proved that the mound was artificial, because they could not have got into such a position otherwise. The search for the tomb-chambers could now proceed with some confidence. What had happened was that water had at some time entered the lower levels of the mound and the subterranean chambers, and its action had transformed the ancient mud-brick into a very hard congealed mass. Working through such stuff was extremely difficult, and when objects began to appear, they had to be removed from the ground by slow and careful picking with knives—a technique which had to be learned by the Quftis who were used to working in loose earth or sand.

For the remainder of the 1931–32 season, and for the whole of the following season, work continued at Ballana. The gang was increased to four hundred men, and a light railway was installed to carry away the great quantities of earth removed from the tumuli. In March 1933 Emery and his party returned to Cairo to work on their material in the Museum. Unexpectedly it was learned that the heightening of the Aswan Dam was ahead of schedule. Archaeological work in Nubia had to be completed by March 1934. Emery therefore had no option but to return to Ballana immediately. The prospect of spending the months of April, May and June in Nubia was not very inviting, but their ordeal in the summer heat was not to pass unrewarded.

For their first task they settled on a relatively modest mound which they numbered Tomb 80. When a large part of the tumulus had been removed they found that the rock-like state of the ground below was particularly difficult to work, and it was at first impossible to discover where walls and chambers were. By chance they struck down initially into the actual burial chambers, and found that it contained an intact burial. All the contents of the room were welded into a solid mass by hard mud, and the disentangling of what was there became a slow and arduous process. Gradually an extraordinary collection of material was recovered. The body of the king or chieftain had been laid on a wooden bed which had long ago collapsed. In death he had worn a silver crown on his head, necklaces of semi-precious stones around his neck, silver bracelets on his arms; between his legs was an iron sword in a silver scabbard. At the head of the bed was the skeleton of a large dog, and nearby were the remains of a camel and of a man who seemed to have died with his arms raised up as if to shield his head from the blow that killed him. The burial-chamber contained two more human skeletons and a number of silver and iron weapons, vessels of bronze and a bronze folding stool.

A second chamber contained the body of a woman who was probably the chieftain's wife, surrounded by the skeletons of her

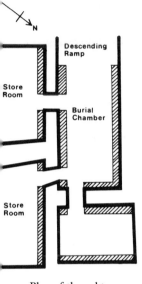

Plan of the subterranean chambers in Tomb 80 at Ballana

Hinged silver bracelets set with onyx, beryls, amethysts and garnets from the tomb of a queen at Ballana.

ladies. She too wore a silver crown embellished with carnelians and decorated with debased Egyptian designs. Two further rooms were packed with all kinds of objects which would have been of use in the after-life: bronze vessels, lamps, tripods, tables, pottery containers of many kinds, some with very attractive decoration, and large quantities of iron weapons and tools and unworked ingots of the metal, ready to be made into things in the next world. On the ramp leading to the burial chambers were the expected horses and camels, but no silver trappings were found. This burial, intact as it was, served as an illustration of what most of the tombs had been like originally; but it was less rich and smaller than those found plundered at Qustol. It could be imagined what would have been buried with the chieftains who had occupied the Qustol tombs.

After Tomb 80 several other virtually intact tombs were excavated at Ballana, but work continued only with difficulty. The strain of working in temperatures rarely falling below 110°F in the daytime, slowly impaired the efficiency of the team, and even the Egyptian workmen found it too hot. They were even obliged to wear shoes because of the heat of the ground, and this was a considerable disadvantage to men who normally wore nothing on their feet. Still, much valuable material was carefully recovered, and not the least remarkable burial belonged to a woman, probably a queen or a princess. She wore a silver crown of very elaborate design; twenty bracelets encircled her arms, some of silver only, others of silver set with semi-precious stones; around her neck were a massive silver collar and fourteen necklaces; on each side of her head were nine silver ear-rings, variously inlaid and decorated; her fingers and toes were fitted with many rings, and seven anklets of silver and coral decorated her legs. It was small wonder that the excavators irreverently called this woman 'Jingling Millie'.

In early June Emery and his team left Ballana for the last time. They had done all they could, at a galloping pace and in extreme conditions. They had revealed the extraordinary riches of the rulers of a barbaric people. Thirty years later a third campaign to investigate the antiquities of Nubia was begun. This time a new and much higher dam was to be built a few miles to the south of the old Aswan Dam. It would create a great lake stretching for hundreds of miles southwards, flooding the whole of Egyptian Nubia and part of Sudanese Nubia. All ancient sites would be submerged, and all the temples, built or rock-cut in the region, would be lost under the waters, unless they were moved. Again Emery was a principal figure in the planning and execution of the campaign. By now he had become a professor in London University, and he excavated on behalf of the Egypt Exploration Society of London. Many nations co-operated with the Antiquities Services of Egypt and the Sudan in the biggest archaeological enterprise ever mounted. The whole of the threatened area was surveyed once again, and the sites needing excavation were allotted to the expeditions of the participating nations. After the work of the earlier surveys most of the sites remaining were of very late date or of uncertain interest. Some expeditions found little; others were well rewarded for their efforts, although no great treasures were discovered. In addition, all the temples were moved to positions which would be well above the expected level of the new lake. Some had to be cut out of the cliffs, like the great temples of Ramesses II at Abu Simbel. The successful extraction of these monuments from their rock-cut sites was a triumph of engineering. Emery himself excavated a small X-group cemetery in Egyptian Nubia, and a great Middle Kingdom fortress in Sudanese Nubia. But nothing was found quite like the burials of Ballana and Qustol, and nothing was found which made the identity of the X-group peoples any clearer. The problem now may never be solved for the waters of Lake Nasser cover the X-group realm.

POSTSCRIPT

Some secrets will ever elude the archaeologist's spade. Others will in time surely be made clear as more sites are dug and better methods of interpretation developed. People often ask, 'Is there more to be discovered in Egypt?' The answer is certainly 'Yes! Perhaps more than has been discovered up to the present.' This answer does not mean that the discoveries of the future will necessarily be as dramatic as some of those described in this book. But there are areas of Egypt which have only partially been explored. The Delta is largely unknown; the site of the great city of Memphis has hardly been touched; few town sites in general have been examined. In the past archaeologists working in Egypt have mostly concentrated on tombs and necropolis areas because they lie above the water line and are relatively easy to dig. Tombs also tend to be productive of interesting and beautiful objects. By the application of new techniques of excavation it should be possible in the future to explore many of the town and village sites more profitably than was possible in the past. This exploration may also be helped by the new stability of the water table in Egypt resulting from the construction of the new High Dam.

But what are the chances of finding another tomb as rich as that of Tutankhamun? Unhappily, not very great. Most of the undiscovered royal tombs belong to periods when burials were not carried out at Thebes, and it is unlikely that the conditions anywhere else in Egypt would result in the splendid state of preservation found in tombs in the Valley of the Kings. Excavation, however, is full of surprises, and it would be rash to declare that wonderful treasures will never again be found in Egypt. On the other hand, Egyptologists may look forward to many less sensational discoveries which will fill up some of the gaps in our knowledge of ancient Egyptian history and life. They may also expect to learn much by the reinterpretation of material already discovered through the application of new scientific methods of examination. They may hope, for example, to find out more about what happened in the dark ages of the First and Second Intermediate Periods, and in the Late New Kingdom when so much must have been going on of which little is known. Whether they work in the field or in the study, Egyptologists undoubtedly have many excitements to expect in the years to come.

BOOKS FOR FURTHER READING

BUDGE, E. A. W., The Rosetta Stone (British Museum, London 1929)

CARTER, H. and MACE, A. C., The Tomb of Tut-Ankh-Amen, 3 vols (Cassell, London 1923–33)

EDWARDS, I. E. S., The Pyramids of Egypt (Penguin, Harmondsworth 1947)

EMERY, W. B., Nubian Treasure (Methuen, London 1948)

GARDINER, A. H., Egypt of the Pharaohs (Oxford University Press, London 1961)

GONEIM, Z., The Buried Pyramid (Longmans, London 1956)

GREENER, L., The Discovery of Egypt (Cassell, London 1966)

A general Introductory Guide to the Egyptian Collections in the British Museum (London 1964)

PETRIE, W. M. F., Seventy Years in Archaeology (S. Low, London 1931)

POSENER, G., A Dictionary of Egyptian Civilisation (Methuen, London 1962)

REISNER, G. A., History of the Giza Necropolis II (The Tomb of Hetep-heres the Mother of Cheops), (Harvard University Press, Cambridge, Mass. 1955)

WINLOCK, H. E., Models of Daily Life in Ancient Egypt (Harvard University Press, Cambridge, Mass. 1955)

INDEX